The Best of Coaching Volleyball, Book II:
The Advanced Elements of the Game

Edited by Kinda S. Asher

MASTERS PRESS

A Division of Howard W. Sams & Co.
A Bell Atlantic Company

Published by Masters Press
(A Division of Howard W. Sams & Co., A Bell Atlantic Company)
2647 Waterfront Pkwy. E. Dr., Suite 300
Indianapolis, IN 46214

Published 1996

Printed in the United States of America

Library of Congress Cataloging-in-Publication Data

The best of coaching volleyball series of handbooks / American Volleyball Coaches Association.
      p.   cm.
   Includes bibliographical references and indexes.
   Contents: [1] Basic elements of the game -- [2] Advanced elements of the game -- [3] Related elements of the game.
     ISBN 1-570238-083-5 (v.1). -- ISBN 1-57028-08403 (v.2). -- ISBN 1-57028-085-1 (v.3).
    1. Volleyball --Coaching--Handbooks, manuals, etc. I. American Volleyball Coaches Association. II. Coaching volleyball.

GV1015.5.C63B47   1996   95-43827
796.325--dc20   CIP

The Best of Coaching Volleyball, Book II: The Advanced Elements of the Game

Credits:
Cover design by Dennis Kugizaki, Kugizaki Design Inc., Colorado
    Springs, Colo.
Text design by Kevin Kaneshiro
Cover photo: University of Southern California sports information
    office/photographic services
Cover coach: Lisa Love, head women's volleyball coach, University of
    Southern California

Table of Contents

Acknowledgements   vi

Preface   ix

Section I - The Serve
    Chapter 1 - The Jump Serve - H. Scott Strohmeyer, Ph.D.   1
    Chapter 2 - The Jump Serve: An Emphasis on Physics - Roger Thinnes   7
    Chapter 3 - Developing Mental Skills While Serving - Ronnie Lidor, Ph.D.   13

Section II - The Attack
    Chapter 4 - Elements of the Back-Row Attack - Andy Banachowski   19
    Chapter 5 - Setter and Quick Hitter Efficiency - Mark Pavlik   25
    Chapter 6 - One Leg Up on the Opposition - Sean Madden   31
    Chapter 7 - The Right Side Attack - Joey Vrazel   39
    Chapter 8 - Splitting the Block - Gary Redenbacher   45

Section III - The Block
    Chapter 9 - The Evaluation of Blocking - Jim Coleman, Ph.D.   51
    Chapter 10 - Blocking at the Collegiate Level - Greg Giovanazzi   57

Section IV - Serve Receive
    Chapter 11 - The Diagonal System of Serve Receive - Kathryn L. Davis, Ph.D.   63
    Chapter 12 - The Philosophy of the Match-Up - Terry Liskevych, Ph.D.   67
    Chapter 13 - Siding Out With a Two- or Three-Person Receive - Bob Maxwell   73
    Chapter 14 - Utilizing Yor Best Receivers in Each Rotation - Chuck Braden   77

Section V - Defense
    Chapter 15 - Developing and Communicating About Defenses - Sean Madden   83
    Chapter 16 - Motivation for Floor Defense - Mike Welch   95

Section VI - Drills
    Chapter 17 - Transition Drills - Tom Shoji   103
    Chapter 18 - Two Competitive Team Drills - Tom Read   105
    Chapter 19 - Volleyball Mini-Games and Movement Training - Don Shondell,
        Ph.D./Joel Walton   109
    Chapter 20 - Bonusball - Joel Dearing   117
    Chapter 21 - The Run Through - Brenda Williams   121

Contributors

Authors

Andy Banachowski, head women's coach, University of California Los Angeles (Los Angeles, Calif.)

Chuck Braden, volleyball coach, New Knoxville Volleyball Club (New Knoxville, Ohio)

Jim Coleman, Ph.D., director, National Teams Training Center (San Diego, Calif.)

Kathryn L. Davis, Ph.D., associate professor, North Carolina State University (Raleigh, N.C.)

Joel Dearing, head women's and men's coach, Springfield College (Springfield, Mass.)

Greg Giovanazzi, head women's coach, University of Michigan (Ann Arbor, Mich.)

Ronnie Lidor, Ph.D., director, Research and Data Analysis Department, The Zinman College of Physical Education at the Wingate Institute Ltd. (Israel)

Terry Liskeych, Ph.D., head coach, U.S. women's national team (San Diego, Calif.)

Sean Madden, head women's coach, Gonzaga University (Spokane, Wash.)

Bob Maxwell, head women's coach, State University of New York, Buffalo (Buffalo, N.Y.)

Mark Pavlik, head men's coach, Penn State University (University Park, Pa.)

Tom Read, physical education instructor, California's Saddleback Valley Unified School District

Gary Redenbacher, former volleyball coach at Fresno State (Fresno, Calif.), and current attorney in Santa Cruz, Calif.

Tom Shoji, head women's coach, University of Southern Colorado (Pueblo, Colo.)

Don Shondell, Ph.D., head men's coach, Ball State University (Muncie, Ind.)

*H. Scott Strohmeyer, Ph.D., Exercise and Sport Sciences (earned at the University of North Carolina at Greensboro in Greensboro, N.C.)

Roger Thinnes, head women's coach, Highland Community College (Freeport, Ill.)

Joey Vrazel, head women's coach, Purdue University (West Lafayette, Ind.)

Joel Walton, assistant men's coach, Ball State University (Muncie, Ind.)

Mike Welch, head women's coach, University of North Florida (Jacksonville, Fla.)

Brenda Williams, director, Divers Sports Center Volleyball Club (Manteno, Ill.)

Editors

General Editor: Kinda Asher, director of publications, American Volleyball Coaches Association

Copy Editors: Sandra Vivas and Vivian Langley, American Volleyball Coaches Association

Advisors

Darlene Kluka, Ph.D., assistant professor, University of Central Oklahoma

Sean Madden, head women's coach, Gonzaga University

Geri Polvino, Ph.D., head women's coach, Eastern Kentucky University

Don Shondell, Ph.D., head men's coach, Ball State University

Sandra Vivas, executive director, American Volleyball Coaches Association

*coaching position at the time the article was first published in *Coaching Volleyball.*

Acknowledgements

In today's world, the measure of true success is seen in the compilation. Professional musicians release "best of" CDs, while actors and actresses are judged by the body of their work, as are authors and researchers. Indeed, if a particular person, event or publication has been around long enough — and has been successful enough — to warrant a "collection," there is a demand for the product. Since 1987, there has been a demand for *Coaching Volleyball*, the official technical journal of the American Volleyball Coaches Association, and now the best the publication has to offer can be found in a new series of books.

The *Best of Coaching Volleyball* series (Books I-III) was the brainchild of the *Coaching Volleyball* Editorial Board and the AVCA office staff. The AVCA is continually searching for innovative avenues to serve its members from an educational standpoint; the *Best of Coaching Volleyball* series is one of the many innovations.

The project could not have begun without the Editorial Board, specifically Darlene Kluka, Ph.D. (assistant professor, University of Central Oklahoma), Sean Madden (head women's coach, Gonzaga University), Geri Polvino, Ph.D. (head women's volleyball coach, Eastern Kentucky) and Don Shondell, Ph.D. (head men's volleyball coach, Ball State University), without whose expertise and patience this publication would have floundered. In addition, the AVCA membership itself must be praised, as it is the members of the organization — the coaches of all levels — who provide the articles for *Coaching Volleyball* on a consistent basis. Without their willingness to share ideas on this ever changing sport, the journal itself would not exist. The coaches who are also USA Volleyball Coaching Accreditation Program (CAP) accredited coaches strive continually to "shake up" the volleyball world with innovative new techniques and tactics.

Undeniably, the heartiest thanks must go to the 21 coaches whose works appear in this publication. Revisions and fine tuning of these articles was a responsibility thrust upon them — and each took the challenge to heart.

Finally, many thanks go to Tom Bast, publisher, Holly Kondras, editor, and the rest of the Masters Press staff for their support and expertise throughout the varied stages of this project. The first book in the series, *The Best of Coaching Volleyball, Book One: The Basic Elements of the Game*, continues to enjoy phenomenal success. *Book Two* will surely follow in its ground breaking footsteps.

Kinda S. Asher, Editor
AVCA Director of Publications
March 1996

Preface

Eight years ago, the American Volleyball Coaches Association recognized the need for a technical journal specifically designed for volleyball coaches of all levels, from junior/club to international. As a result, *Coaching Volleyball* was born.

Today, *Coaching Volleyball* serves as the leading periodical devoted to the technical aspects of the game. The journal is read bi-monthly by more than 3,000 AVCA members and subscribers, both domestic and international. The demand for technically correct information on coaching and learning the sport has inspired the AVCA to compile the best articles from the technical journal and showcase them in a series of three publications. The *Best of Coaching Volleyball* series (Books I-III) is the response to that need.

In this, the second book of the series, experienced coaches and players are treated to 21 chapters discussing the advanced elements of the game of volleyball. Coaches from all levels -- and from all around the country- - offer their ideas on how to teach the serve, the attack, the block, etc. It is truly an eclectic combination of information geared to the coach or player well-versed in the intricacies of the sport of volleyball.

The book is divided into six sections:

Section I   The Serve
Section II   The Attack
Section III   The Block
Section IV   Serve Receive
Section V   Defense
Section VI   Drills

Twenty-one coaches have offered their varied expertise on the sport of volleyball. Each chapter is rife with photos, graphics and diagrams to aid the reader in understanding and grasping the material. In addition, a number of the chapters pull related information from other sources to provide the reader with an even broader base of information. Indeed, the *Best of Coaching Volleyball* series is unlike any volleyball publication you have read.

Kinda S. Asher, Editor
AVCA Director of Publications

Section I: The Serve

The Jump Serve

The Jump Serve

H. Scott Strohmeyer

The emergence of the jump serve in volleyball in the 1980s has added a new dimension to the game. In essence, a jump serving volleyball team is now capable of attacking when putting the ball in play. In fact, some of the best jump servers in the world are actually getting a free hit to begin play. In a study conducted regarding the jump servers of the men's and women's national volleyball teams, attacking on serve is exactly what was happening. I remember analyzing the data for this study in complete disbelief of one jump serve that Karch Karaly executed. It was quite remarkable that this serve traveled at just over 23 m/s (52 mph), but what was even more surprising, at the time, was that this serve never went up. That is, from the point of contact to its landing in the opposing court, this serve was hit down. One can imagine, then, the importance of studying the jump serve to determine what the important variables are for training others to execute the skill effectively.

This article is the result of one small study which has tried to examine the important teaching variables of the jump serve. All of the numeric data presented is available as a result of 16mm film records taken of five members of the 1988 Olympic teams and was analyzed at the U.S. Olympic Training Center in Colorado Springs, Colo. The instructional cues relayed in this article are the result of long hours of qualitative analysis of these athletes and many other jump servers, both nationally and internationally. It is my goal not to write a definitive view of the jump serve and its technique, but to examine otherwise this sport and its techniques objectively and relay these findings more quickly to the coach.

Photo: James Sefton

According to Strohmeyer, the jump serve gives a team an advantage because the higher velocities of the ball give the defense less time to react to the ball's flight path. If reaction to the serve trajectory is not as efficient, the pass off serve has a greater chance of being poor.

ADVANTAGES

The jump serve is appealing for use in competition for a variety of reasons. First, the server can create greater forces, due to the increased range of motion inherent to this serve. This allows the ball to travel at greater velocities than the conventional overhand serve. The subjects in our study were jump serving the volleyball with an average velocity of 19 m/s (42.5 mph). The conventional servers were serving at an average velocity of 14 m/s (31 mph). These differences are significant not only statistically, but also as an attacking tool for the offense. The higher velocities of the ball give the defense less time to react to its flight path. If reaction to the serve trajectory is not as efficient, the pass off serve has a greater chance of being poor. Thus, the attack off serve reception may not be as effective. The second appealing factor of the jump serve is that the jump allows the server to serve at lower trajectory angles (approximately six degrees above horizontal for the jump serve as compared to 13 degrees above horizontal for the conventional overhand serve) because the server is contacting the volleyball at an elevated hitting position. Conceptually, this is appealing because the serve receiver must then direct the ball with slightly more loft than normal to get the ball into position for the setter. Thus, the jump serve has the potential not only to diminish the time the receivers have to react, but also to change a preferred movement pattern of the receiver.

The start position for the jump serve varies from 3 to 4.6 m (10-15 ft.) from the endline, depending on the server's stride. The jump serve has a pre-contact approach, as in spiking, which leads into a vertical jump. Once a start position is established, the toss and approach should be learned. The toss [should be initiated with one hand]. The toss has to be high enough and moving sufficiently in the direction of the server's endline to allow enough time for the server to make an approach and takeoff. After the coordination and timing of the toss are mastered, the height of the toss is the biggest problem for proper execution of the jump serves (as it is for all serves). The mechanics of spiking also apply to jump serving with one exception: the contact with the ball. Contact should be the heel-snap contact, but it needs to occur below the midpoint of the ball, ensuring a curved trajectory that passes well above the net [but not as high as the conventional overhand serve would].

(Gambardella, Bob. (1987.) Serving. *The AVCA Volleyball Handbook.* Indianapolis, IN: Master's Press, 83-84.)

An often overlooked advantage of the jump serve is that the jump serve, when executed correctly, will carry the server onto the court, ready for play. This helps avoid the scenario where our server watches the serve and is late getting into proper defensive position.

Finally, an often overlooked advantage of the jump serve is that the jump serve, when executed correctly, will carry the server onto the court, ready for play. This helps avoid the scenario where our server watches the serve and is late getting into proper defensive position. These advantages of the jump serve, though not comprehensive, are also not without disadvantages.

DISADVANTAGES

The most notable disadvantage of the jump serve is that the jump serve tends to be less accurate than the conventional overhand serve.

In this study, the subjects were asked to execute the respective serve until 10 playable serves were achieved. Accuracy was computed by dividing the 10 playable serves by the total amount of serves needed. The jump servers were accurate approximately 72 percent of the time, while the conventional overhand servers were accurate 80 percent of the time. The difference here does not seem to be significant. However, if we remember that these are all athletes competing at the international level, the difference in accuracy between the two serves will only increase as the ability levels of our performers decrease.

The decreased accuracy of the jump serve lies in a variety of areas. First, the jump serve is much more dynamic than the conventional serve. Moving through a wide range to execute the jump serve introduces timing parameters that are not normally inherent to the conventional overhand serve. Not only does the server need to jump to serve, but a toss must also be made by the server to his/herself and that toss is traveling away from the server.

Second, although the effects of fatigue were not determined, the author has observed that the use of the jump serve declines as match progresses. This may be a direct result of fatigue or an acknowledgment that accuracy is a necessity as time passes in a match.

These disadvantages, though they may seem overwhelming, have been derived from a relatively new skill to the sport of volleyball. The author believes that much of the timing—and therefore accuracy problems inherent to the jump serve at this time—may be remedied if we can convince junior high and high school physical educators and coaches to introduce this skill to their athletes.

I have begun teaching the jump serve to athletes as young as 13 years of age and it is now a common feature in all of my beginning level volleyball courses and theory of coaching courses.

THE TOSS

The jump serve begins with the ball toss, which in many ways is the most important part of the serve. In the complete jump serve, the toss should begin approximately 10-12 feet behind the endline. Ideally, according to Newton's Laws of Motion, the toss should be executed with one hand (creating forces on the toss that act only in the intended direction of flight). Of the subjects tested for this study, only Eric Sato and Karch Kiraly did this. The other performers in the study seemed to rely on what seemed to be most comfortable for them. The toss should be made toward the court in such a manner that it reaches its peak trajectory approximately 1-3 feet before reaching the endline. A consistent toss is one key to becoming a good jump server.

APPROACH

The approach of the jump server should only be slightly angled (at most) if not perpendicular to the court. This will allow the server to use all available court surface on the opponent's side of the net. The athletes in this study approached the jump serve with a four or a slightly modified four-step approach. The modified four-step approach was characterized by two short steps, followed by a long step and an incomplete step into the plant phase of the jump. The preparatory armswing used on the approach to the jump serve should mirror the preparatory armswing the athlete uses when executing the hit at the net.

GATHER OR PLANT PHASE

The most difficult part of the jump serve to teach has been the gather or plant phase. Not unlike the hit at the net, the gather phase of the jump serve should be a smooth transition phase from the horizontal component of the approach to the verticality of the actual jump. However, contrary to the plant phase when hitting at the net, the jump serve uses a pronounced front-back stride of approximately 15-18 inches in length. In the hit at the net, the feet are staggered very little. This front-back stride will help propel the server forward into the serve.

The subjects in this study were contacting the ball when they were approximately 20-30 inches over the court. This becomes very attractive to the strategist when one considers that not only is the serve moving faster, but the server has also shortened the court, thereby further decreasing the time allotted the receiver to react to the serve. Also, by having the server moving into the ball, the momentum of the server's body will allow greater force to be imparted to the ball without increasing the velocity of the armswing through contact. If the jump server is jumping straight up or backwards, the added momentum is negated and the resultant velocity of the served ball is no different than if the server were serving from the ground. Again, preparatory armswing through this phase of the jump serve, as well as through ball contact, is identical to the hit at the net.

CONTACT OF THE BALL

Contact of the ball should occur when the server is at the peak of her/his jump. This is the point of slowest vertical movement of the athlete's body. Again, this is similar to the hit at the net. The follow-through after ball contact may be more exaggerated than the hit because the server

Newton's first law states that anything that is not moving will remain that way unless an external force is applied to it. This also implies that anything which is moving will not stop moving unless something stops it. Simply, Newton said that bodies which have mass also have inertia. (Inertia is a relative measure of an object's mass.) More generally, it describes the reluctance of an object to change its state of motion. The more massive the object, the more reluctant the object is to change its state of motion.

(Vint, Peter. Citius, altius, fortius. *Coaching Volleyball*, October/November 1993, 27.)

does not need to worry about a net violation. Remember also, that the athlete should be jumping onto the court.

The most common misconception that most beginning jump servers have is that they feel they must swing the arm through the ball harder than when they serve conventionally. Convincing them that their body's momentum will increase the ball's velocity alone will speed the server's progress. Adding power to the armswing, if necessary, can be incorporated at a later time. Early in a server's development it is enough just to become consistent at executing this new movement pattern.

> The most common misconception that most beginning jump servers have is that they feel they must swing the arm through the ball harder than when they serve conventionally. Convincing them that their body's momentum will increase the ball's velocity alone will speed the server's progress.

In the years since the jump serve's "emergence" in competitive volleyball, I have noticed a developmental sequence that many jump servers go through when refining their own vertical jump. Most jump servers who learn the jump serve on their own build into the full skill literally one step at a time. The first attempts at jump serving take the form of a short toss, with no approach before jumping. Once competency has been gained with the rudimentary jump serve, the need for a more powerful serve leads the server into a one-step approach. This progression will continue until the jump server is confident in the whole process outlined above. I have not seen a competent jump server, as yet, execute more than four steps on the approach. This progression of development of skill acquisition may be useful for the instructor of performers who may not be able to manipulate fully the dynamic nature of the whole serve upon first try.

How will I know if a server has the jump serve down well enough for game play? This is a question you will have to answer for yourself. In general, however, I will look for the athlete whose toss is probably consistent enough to allow for accuracy in the serve.

*At the time the article was first published in *Coaching Volleyball*, H. Scott Strohmeyer was a Ph.D. candidate in exercise sport and sciences at the University of North Carolina at Greensboro, N.C.

The Jump Serve: An Emphasis on Physics

The Jump Serve: An Emphasis on Physics

The jump serve has been around since the 1960s (Selinger, 1986), but remained in obscurity until television brought the excitement into the home. Teaching the jump serve requires the emphasis of certain key points. First this article will examine two basic rules for all types of serves. Then some mathematical number crunching will shed some light on the physical requirements of the jump serve. Finally, a teaching model is presented for coaches to use with their players.

According to Thinnes, what the body parts do prior to or following contact have no influence on the ball. Actual contact of the ball with the hand is the only time force can be imparted.

TWO SERVING RULES

Before discussing any serve, the critical point must be identified. This critical point is contact with the ball. What the body parts do prior to or following contact have no influence on the ball. Actual contact of the ball with the hand is the only time force can be imparted. The following two rules are actually teaching cues that reinforce proper ball contact.

More than a decade ago, David DeGroot (personal communication) pointed out that there are two rules for serving: 1) palm to the target and 2) look down your arm after contact. Whether the serve is underhand, overhand floater, Asian floater, overhand topspin, roundhouse topspin or jump serve, these axioms hold true for all types of serves.

If a coach has a player who shanks the serve or has accuracy trouble, observe carefully the direction the palm is facing at contact. Next, have the player hit the serve and sight down the hitting arm. The arm will be pointing toward the ball as it flies away.

The observation technique is somewhat more difficult for the roundhouse and the jump serve because of the magnitude of the follow-through. Even so, the two rules mentioned above will always be followed by the ball.

THE JUMP SERVE - PROJECTILE KINETICS

Database searches have revealed only one relevant research paper on the jump serve. The paper, by Strohmeyer (1988), published values of initial ball velocity and angle of projection for Olympic-caliber jump servers. The mean initial velocity (Vri) for females is 18.06 m/s with a mean angle of projection (q) of 6.10° (Strohmeyer, 1988). As a result, the ball is moving upward at Vy = 1.919 m/s. Simultaneously, the ball is moving away from the server at Vx=17.958m/s. Figure 1 shows the results of projectile analysis using equations by Northrip, Logan and McKinney (1983) and values by Strohmeyer (1988), with an arbitrary contact point directly above the endline. The minimum height of the initial contact (ho) with the given Vri and q that allows the ball to clear the 2.24 m net by one inch and still land in bounds is 2.64 m. This converts to ho = 8'8".

In Figure 2, the contact point was arbitrarily moved 1 meter behind the endline. Visual ob-

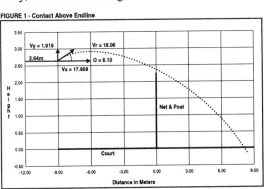

FIGURE 1 - Contact Above Endline

Vy = 1.919   Vr = 18.06
2.64m   Θ = 6.10
Vx = 17.958

Net & Post

Court

Height in Meters

Distance in Meters

8

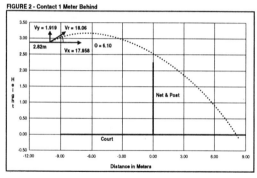

FIGURE 2 - Contact 1 Meter Behind

servation of jump servers of less-than-Olympic-caliber indicates contact takes place somewhere behind the endline. If the same initial conditions (Vri = 18.06 and q = 6.10°) are used, then the minimum ho = 2.82 m = 9'3". This represents an increase of 7 inches in the minimum contact height if the same serve was contacted only one meter behind the endline. Coaches can accurately infer that as the distance behind the endline is increased, the minimum ho rises dramatically.

IMPLICATIONS

For the jump serve to be most effective, the angle of projection should be minimal, the contact point should be as high as possible and the velocity as fast as possible. The jump serve is not suited for everybody. After analyzing the indicated parameters, any athlete unable to contact the ball at the minimum ho and with the given velocity is wasting valuable time and energy.

TEACHING THE JUMP SERVE - A MODEL

When teaching the jump serve to those with the identified physical readiness, coaches should borrow the teaching mode presented by Dr. Gary Wiren (1990). Even though Wiren's model is related to golf, the premise applies to the jump serve.

For the jump serve to be most effective, the angle of projection should be minimal, the contact point should be as high as possible and the velocity as fast as possible.

Wiren's model indicates three ideas occur in the teaching model: 1) laws, 2) principles, and 3) preferences.

LAWS

The laws Wiren refers to are the laws of nature or the laws of physics, which are unyielding. These laws occur each and every time the skill is executed and follow a rigid, predictable outcome. An example of this is the projectile kinetics discussed a few paragraphs earlier. The equations used to calculate ho are results of the law of uniform acceleration. Neglecting air resistance, an object falls to Earth under the influence of gravity at the rate of 9.8 m/s or 32 c/s (Northrip, et al., 1983).

Because of this law, the ball follows a predictable trajectory based on initial conditions.

PRINCIPLES

Principles are true statements relating variables and their changes to the laws. Mathematically, equations become the shorthand versions of principles. Principles give the coach a method of determining how a change in a single variable will affect the outcome when the law is applied. The principle used earlier stated that for a given set of initial conditions, as the contact of the serve is moved farther from the net, the minimum contact point for a successful serve is raised. If the preceding example were repeated without changing ho and the contact point is moved farther from the net, a higher trajectory (q) of serve will be required to avoid a service error. This is counter-productive for the jump serve since the angle of projection needs to be as small as possible.

Since projectiles travel in a parabolic path, nearly every serve in volleyball must be projected upward. The idea that the jump serve allows the server to hit the ball "downward" or "directly over" the net is false (Selinger, 1986). As of this writing, only one subject has a documented serve with a negative angle of inclination (Strohmeyer, 1988). To hit downward consistently, the contact point must be higher than 3.0 meters.

To avoid driving the jump serve into the net, the coach must instruct the athlete on the principles of parabolic flight and teach the player to hit up and through the ball.

PREFERENCES

When Wiren's model is applied to teaching the jump serve, preferences is the area where coaches can disagree and the teaching process may break down. Preferences are individual choices made by coaches and players which still use the principles correctly and ultimately follow the laws. For example, should the ball be lifted with the hitting hand, the opposite hand or with both hands?

Coaches may have their opinions as to which lift is better, but these opinions need to be suppressed if the athlete has more confidence, or better accuracy, using another equally effective method. Forcing a coach's preference on a player using a valid preference disrupts the learning curve. If the player is having problems using their preference, then the coach should present alternative preferences which support the principles.

MECHANICS OF THE JUMP SERVE: LIFTING THE BALL

The purpose of the lift is to put the ball in a location where optimal contact can occur. The mechanism for getting the ball to that location is irrelevant.

A positive case for each of the three legal lifts can be made rather quickly.

• Lifting with the hitting hand-Why would a coach want a player to lift the ball with the non-dominant (and usually weaker) arm? Use the stronger, dominant arm to control the ball

• Lifting with the non-hitting hand-Using transfer of knowledge, relate the lift to the tennis serve. Also, which hand does the lifting in a normal floater serve? Maintain a consistent transfer from one skill to another.

• Using both hands-Players use both hands to toss the ball to the setter in a hitting line. They do this because the toss is more accurate. The lift for the jump serve needs to be accurate, too!

All three lifts have their merit. Let the player have a preference. If the player's lift is causing problems with the serve, then suggest one of the

Although the jump serve was the exciting addition to the 1984 Los Angeles Olympics, its use has been traced back to the 1960s. The jump serve is rather difficult to master because of all of the variables involved in it. Strength, coordination and proper movement are prerequisites to the mastery of the skill. The jump serve produces more points, but at the same time, it can cause lots of errors. A team that is only an average passing team will make more errors when confronted with this type of serve.

(Gambardella, Bob. (1987). Serving. *The AVCA Volleyball Handbook,* Indianapolis, IN: Masters Press, 83.)

other lifts. Now, at this point, the coach can interject her/his personal preference.

APPROACH FOOTWORK

The coach should also transfer this teaching model to the footwork phase of the jump serve. The combined skill of running, lifting, jumping and hitting becomes complicated when each segment must be executed in proper sequence and with proper timing. The athlete needs to choose his/her own preference for the two-step, three-step or four-step approach. Since the footwork pattern is identical to the spike, the player will probably adopt a normal attack approach without any coaching input. Outside hitters will probably prefer a four- or three-step approach, while middle hitters will generally choose a shorter approach. The path of the approach will also vary from straight ahead or diagonal or curvilinear, all of which are just fine; they are only preferences. Coaches should note and instruct the player that each path may affect the location of the serve.

> When teaching a player to hit the jump serve, check to see if that player has the physical readiness to accomplish the jump serve.

BALL CONTACT

Based on the data presented, it is imperative that the jump serve be contacted as close to the net as possible. This will shorten the time of flight and allow a smaller angle of inclination. The coach should accept contact directly above the endline as the minimum standard of performance. Any serves contacted behind the endline are considered unacceptable. The jump serve has so many inherent risks, that even though the contact meets or exceeds the minimum standards, the effectiveness will be greatly magnified if contact is made on or forward of the endline.

SUMMARY

When teaching a player to hit the jump serve, check to see if that player has the physical readiness to accomplish the jump serve. If the player cannot contact the ball at the minimum height and with the necessary projection kinetics, then the player is wasting valuable energy mastering a serve which has a high risk factor. The philosophy behind the jump serve is to disrupt the opponent's serve receive (Selinger, 1986; Strohmeyer, 1988) while accepting a few more errors along the way. Without the minimum physical requirements, the player will use large quantities of energy and still project the ball with the same parameters as a conventional standing serve.

The jump serve is an effective weapon to disrupt the flow of the game and to increase the perceived stress on the serve receivers. The jump serve is an important tactical weapon for high-level teams. Physical readiness is the most important factor when deciding who should learn the jump serve.

The coach should teach and emphasize the principles needed to make full effect of the laws of physics. Personal preferences should be given as alternatives with the coach aiding the athlete in determining a preference that will execute the jump serve most effectively.

REFERENCES

Northrip, J.W., Logan, G.A., & McKinney, W.C. (1983). *Analysis of Sport Motion: Anatomic and Biomechanic Perspectives.* (3rd ed.). Dubuque, IA: Wm C. Brown Company Publishers.

Selinger, A. (1986). *Arie Selinger's Power Volleyball.* New York: Houghton Mifflin Co.

Strohmeyer, H.S. (1988). An analysis of selected cinematographic and descriptive variables in the jump and conventional overhand volleyball serves of the United States Olympic athletes. (Master's thesis, University of Wyoming). Health, Physical Education and Recreation Microform Publications Supplement. 6(2), 2. (University of Oregon Microform No. PE 3082f).

Wiren, G. (1990). Laws, principles and preferences - a teaching model. In Cochran, A.J. (Ed.), *Science and Golf.* Cambridge, U.K.: E & F. N. Spon.

Roger Thinnes is the head women's volleyball coach at Highland Community College in Freeport, Ill., and is a USA Volleyball CAP Level II accredited coach.

Developing Mental Skills While Serving

Developing Mental Skills While Serving RONNIE LIDOR

In volleyball, the serve is one of the most efficient attacking weapons of the game. Initially, the serve is used to put the ball into play. Additionally, it may place the opponents in a weak offensive position or score a direct point. Therefore, coaches should spend a considerable amount of time during practice sessions to enhance this important and fundamental skill.

One of the most common ways in which players can improve their serving ability is to work on some physical components of the skill. For example, players should maintain good posture and keep muscles relaxed, hit the ball at the center of gravity or place the ball about 2 feet above the tossing hand (Hebert, 1991; Viera & Ferguson, 1989). Focusing on these aspects of the serve may result in a better performance.

According to Lidor, when ready to serve the ball, players should not only cope with, but also overcome any psychological barriers.

However, physical components are only one aspect of the skill. Another component to be considered is the cognitive or mental side of the serve. When ready to serve the ball, players should not only cope with, but also overcome any psychological barriers. Psychological phenomena such as stress, anxiety, concentration, focusing attention or fear of failure may increase the mental load on the server, who unfortunately can fail to hit the ball appropriately and successfully.

For years, sport psychologists have been attempting to assist players to strengthen their mental side. Sport psychology and motor learning literature have suggested a variety of techniques that can be implemented by athletes (Nideffer, 1985) to improve psychological preparation prior to and during competitions. One of the techniques described in the literature is to develop learning strategies. By implementing a learning strategy, volleyball players should execute their serves more efficiently and accurately.

WHAT IS A LEARNING STRATEGY?

A learning strategy is defined as an overall plan one formulates before, during and after the performance (Singer, 1988). A strategy is the way a player organizes thoughts when performing a task. It is clear that negative thoughts, for example, can distract a player's attention from the final goal of performance. In contrast, positive thoughts should increase a player's self-confidence, thereby assisting in the attainment of a higher level of proficiency. In a game situation, a volleyball player has five seconds to initiate the serving process. During this period of time, the player can organize thoughts toward the actual performance. Presumably, a learning strategy can be used. One of the learning strategies that has been heavily investigated in the literature under well-controlled laboratory conditions, as well as in field-settings, is the Five Step Approach. This technique was developed by Dr. Robert Singer, a sport psychologist from the University of Florida (1988).

THE FIVE-STEP APPROACH

The Five-Step Approach contains five steps which should be utilized by athletes before, during and after executing a skill. Each of the steps is

Step 1: Be ready mentally and physically to serve the ball.

used independently. However, each one is connected to the previous or the following step. The five steps are basically five sub-strategies, each of which has been recommended as a sport performance enhancement technique in sport psychology. The five steps of the strategy include:

•Step 1: Readying
•Step 2: Imaging
•Step 3: Focusing-attention
•Step 4: Executing
•Step 5: Evaluating

In each step, the player is asked to follow specific procedures. These procedures can be applied during practices, as well as competitions. The prominent characteristics of each of the learning and performance steps are elaborated next.

STEP 1: READYING

Prior to execution of the serve, the player is directed how to control physical and mental states. In this step, the player learns how to be ready for the act of serving.

•Be ready mentally and physically to serve the ball.
•Use similar and, if possible, identical routines before you release the ball.
•Hold the ball and look forward to having a feeling of control in your motion.
•Talk to yourself and guide yourself on how you are going to hit the ball.
•Think positively before you execute the serve.
•Be confident that you are going to serve the ball above the net.
•Implement your own style of serving.
•Do not change your technique at the last minute.

STEP 2: IMAGING

In this step, the volleyball player is guided as to how to create a "mental picture" of the serve to be executed. The player should mentally "see" an effective serve performed.

•Think to yourself that you are going to serve the ball well.
•Think of every aspect of the serve in sequence.
•Imagine the way the ball approaches the net and your opponents.
•Imagine yourself serving the ball and focus your attention.
•Imagine the angle at which on the relevant cue the ball is released from your hands.
•Feel the way you hit the ball.
•Image the exact spot of the opponents' court that the ball is going to hit.

Steps 2 and 3: Imagine yourself serving the ball and focus your attention on the relevant cue.

STEP 3: FOCUSING ATTENTION

While serving the ball, the player is exposed to either internal or external distractions. A player can think negatively (internal impact) or be distracted by auditory effects (external impact). In order to cope efficiently with these distractions, the player should:

•Focus attention on only one relevant cue, which is an integral part of the performance and the environment. For example, the player may focus attention on the ball to be served or at a very specific area of the net.

•Isolate the selected cue from any other cues that may distract your attention.

•When holding the ball prior to execution, focus your attention on the seams of the ball and then shift your attention to the net or to other relevant cues.

•At the end of the act of serving, listen carefully to the sound of the ball hitting your hand. (During this part of the serve, the player can realize if the serve was effectively executed.)

STEP 4: EXECUTION

While serving the ball, the player is directed to clear the mind of any irrelevant thoughts, to let the motion flow and to try to execute rapidly and accurately. Put simply, the player has to execute the serve as though in an automatic mode.

•Serve the ball as automatically as possible.
•Serve the ball using your preferred technique.
•Your serve will be successful.
•Let your serving motion flow.
•Be confident in what you are doing.

Step 4: Serve the ball – "just do it!"

STEP 5: EVALUATION

This is the last step of the strategy and the only one which can be omitted during practices and games. If time permits or the performance situation is fairly comfortable, the player can evaluate the performance and use a self-feedback report for improving the next serve. This step can be used easily in practice sessions and perhaps in real game situations.

•Briefly analyze your serving act.

•If you have performed the serve successfully, try to repeat your performance in the next attempt.

•If you have failed to execute the serve effectively, try to correct your error in the next attempt.

•If required, change your serving strategy.

•Use visual feedback ("what you see"), auditory feedback ("what you hear") and kinesthetic feedback ("what you feel") to improve your serving performance.

PRACTICAL RECOMMENDATIONS FOR VOLLEYBALL COACHES

Coaches should develop appropriate techniques in order to enhance individual and team fundamentals. However, players should not neglect the mental aspects of the game, such as the way players organize their thoughts during specific situations in the game (e.g., serving the ball). In order to assist the coaches in using learning strategies, the following six

Step 5: Evaluate your serving performance (if time permits).

Today we are more aware of various elements of mental traiing as being key to any enhanced level of human performance, including sports. James Loehr states in his book, Mental Toughness Training for Sports, according to many coaches, mental skills encompass anywhere from 50-80 percent of a person's performance. Yet, by most coaches' admission, they use mental skills in only 10-15 percent of practices. Many coaches do not train these skills at all.

(Hockin Ph.D., Robert J. Training the mind. *Coaching Volleyball*, December/January 1993, 28.)

recommendations are worthwhile:

a) Present the main principles of the strategy to the players;

b) Ask the players to implement the strategy during practice sessions;

c) Use simulation techniques during practices in which the strategy can be applied;

d) Remind the players to use the strategy while serving the ball;

e) Try to evaluate the effectiveness of the entire strategy or each one of the five particular steps;

f) Modify the strategy to the specific needs of the player. The strategy should serve the player. If necessary, omit one of the steps or emphasize another. The Five-Step Approach can be adjusted to the individual needs of the player.

SUMMARY

Most volleyball players have their own ways to organize their thoughts while serving the ball. Furthermore, each player has a cognitive style of thinking during the game. Most of the players apply some kind of strategies during practices and games without being aware of the implementation of these beneficial mental processes. However, coaches must also be responsible for the mental side of the game and introduce players to facultative learning. Players should be aware of the positive influence of learning strategies of motor task performance. Consequently, they should be guided in the appreciation of learning strategies during practices and games.

Because the serve is such an important weapon in the modern game, coaches should assist their players in enhancing their abilities to discern, to process information and to make appropriate decisions while serving the ball. It is strongly recommended that the Five Step Approach be incorporated into each practice for greater serving success. Players and coaches should benefit from the implementation of this psychological tool. The server may become more confident, relaxed and focused on performance by using this strategy.

REFERENCES

Hebert, M. (1991). *Insights and Strategies for Wining Volleyball*. Champaign, IL: Leisure Press.

Nideffer, R.M (1985). *Athletes Guide to Sport Training*. Champaign, IL: Human Kinetics.

Singer, R.N. (1988). Strategies and metastrategies in learning and performing self-paced athletic skills. *The Sport Psychologist*, 2, 49-68.

Viera, B.L. and Ferguson, B.J. (1989). *Teaching Volleyball: Steps to Success*, Champaign, IL: Leisure Press.

Ronnie Lidor, Ph.D., is the director of the Research and Data Analysis Department at The Zinman College of Physical Education at the Wingate Institute in Israel.

Section II: The Attack

Elements of the Back-Row Attack

Elements of the Back-Row Attack

ANDY BANACHOWSKI

In volleyball, offensive systems vary greatly, depending on the experience of the team, the power and cunning of individual players and the tack a coach wants to take to see the team perform at its best. Every volleyball team must incorporate an effective front row attack to be competitive. But what about the back-row attack? Andy Banachowski, head women's coach of the UCLA Bruins, offers some advice on including the back-row attack as a viable offensive option.

CV: What do you feel is the significance of the back-row attack in the women's game today?

AB: I think the back-row attack has started to become a much bigger factor for the women as they get more used to using it on offense. The thing that I think is taking so long is that [women] are not quite comfortable with attacking and landing in front of the 3-meter line. Men are much better at it and that is why it is so much more effective for men than for the women. You watch as the women's teams run it—the sets are at 12 feet; they are not setting the ball so that the women broad jump in front of the attack line to hit the set. On the attack, they are so afraid they are going to step on the line or they are not going to have the range to hit it. I think that as they get more comfortable with that, you are going to see a lot more back-row attack. It is going to become a lot more effective. I do not think that it is really as effective in the women's game as it is in the men's game.

CV: Do you concentrate specifically in your practices on developing the back-row attack?

AB: There are a lot of things that we do in our practice drills where we do a lot of back-row hitting, like a three-player exchange drill where there is a lot of back-row attack, forcing the players to set the ball in front of the 3-meter line, hitting the ball where the contact point is in front of the 3-meter line instead of behind [it]. That is the only way they are going to get better at it.

AB: What kind of player do you think is a good back-row attacker, from both a physical and mental standpoint?

AB: I think mentally it would be somebody who is really not afraid to go for the ball. The back-row attack is a play that [an athlete] cannot be timid about. I think for it to be effective, players cannot really be worried about the outcome of the play. They just have to go up and hit the ball because if they are really cautious with it, the ball is going to be dug. Why run an attack where you know the opponents are going to dig the ball? Mentally, we have to have that player who is not afraid to make a mistake and is really willing to go for it.

> Why run an attack where you know the opponents are going to dig the ball? Mentally, we have to have that player who is not afraid to make a mistake and is really willing to go for it.

As far as the physical type of player, you want somebody who can broad jump or long jump when he/she hits. Technically, those are your middle players. You teach your outside hitters that they cannot broad jump, otherwise they are going to get caught underneath the ball; now,

Banachowski believes a good back-row hitter is a person who is not afraid to go for the ball.

Photo: University of Iowa

Two skills are executed in the back-row attack: the set, which provides the ball for the attack and the attack itself.

The set should be high (5 meters or more) and just in front of the attack line. This set is accomplished technically the same as other sets. Its height, placement and consistency are keys to the attack's success. The attacking player should get the set in the same place each time. Because of the greater distance from the net, the spiker has a slimmer margin for error and less ability to adjust to setting errors. A consistent set reduces the chance of an unsuccessful attack.

The back-row attack does have minor changes from the standard attack spike. Most important are the approach and the point of contact. The player approaches powerfully and has a slightly more forward motion on take-off than in the standard attack.

The player jumps up and forward from behind the attack line, meeting the ball at the height of the jump. This should be just in front of the attack line. Arching the back slightly more than normal allows the player to hit powerfully through and over the ball. A powerful double arm swing on take-off helps the player gain the maximum height, the proper forward motion and the back arch needed for the attack.

(Gordon, Don. The back-row attack. *Coaching Volleyball*, August/September 1988, 25.)

for the back-row attack, it changes the rules on them. You do not usually have outside hitters broad jump. Your middle blocker is usually more of a broad jumper, moving horizontally along the net; so they should be the ones who can make the easy transition to the back-court attack (but they are not used to hitting the high ball). There are some different techniques and talents that maybe you look for. [For the most part, a coach should look for] a well-rounded volleyball player to hit back row.]

CV: Coaches used to teach attackers to jump vertically when approaching the net. Now they seem to be jumping forward more — why?

AB: I think that it has to do with the advent of a lot of teams using the swing type of offense where the players are coming from every which way. They have to do so much more correcting with this jump. Three or four years ago, you did not see much of a swing type of offense and the horizontal movement along the net was not so varied.

CV: When you incorporate the back-row attack, how much of your offensive system does it encompass? If it is a major part of your offense, do you leave it up to the setters or the hitters to make the call?

AB: Different coaches have different perspectives. I always let our setters run the offense unless I do not like what they are doing and then I will interject. We will talk about what we want to try to do before the match and then I always feel it is their call to run the game out there. I do not want to be calling specific sets because the setter is the one who has the ball in her hands and has to make the decision as to what to do. There are some things that we try to do before the match to decide whether we want to overload an area or isolate an area. Most of the time it is preferable to try to isolate a little bit, so maybe you want to run all of your hitters to one side of the court and set the back-row attack to the opposite side. Another thing you can do is split your front-row hitters and open up the middle of the court to try to get the opponent's blockers going the wrong way. In order to take advantage of the split in the blockers, you must be willing to run a back-row attack with a lower set, not a skyball. Too many times, players set a skyball so the middle blocker has time to go outside the block and come back to set up the block on the back-court attacker. These are all things you do in practice [to work on your back-row attack].

CV: Do you do any work on coverage if the back-row attack is blocked?

AB: Do not get blocked! Realistically, if a player is blocked, the only person who has a chance of covering is the setter and possibly the quick attacker, depending on whether you split or whether you overload to the side and set back. Probably the only person who has a chance to cover that one is the setter.

CV: That is probably where the setter's decision comes into play as far as what she has seen happening with the blockers and where they are going. Is that correct?

AB: Right. She is also the only one who knows where the ball is going, so she should be the primary one to be able to cover on that play. Plus, the hitters themselves have jumped into a zone where you would expect the ball to be blocked down and she still could cover herself. There are some times when you cannot really establish a typical hitter coverage that you are used to seeing, especially if you want all five players involved. It is just not realistic. Theoretically, yes, but realistically, no.

CV: How do you teach the basics —the mechanics—of the back-row attack?

AB: [An attack from the back row] is just like a normal spike. I think the attack point has to be a little bit more above the shoulder than out front. A player cannot get away with hitting the ball straight down because there is 6 to 8 feet the ball has to travel before it crosses the net. So, it is important to have them reaching for the ball, attacking the ball higher, giving them more of an opportunity to get the ball over the net. When we begin our work and try to determine our [system], we always try to set the ball as far forward in front of the line to find out which players can hit the ball in that position. We try to find where their best attack point is.

Some players can handle it way out in front; others, no matter how much you want them to hit the ball at 7 feet, they are more effective hitting at the 10-foot line because they cannot jump forward. They can jump up really well, but they cannot jump forward.

CV: If you were taking a high school group that was trying to start training individuals in the back-row attack, do you have any suggestions for the coaches at that level?

AB: [At the high school level], if I were a coach, I would concentrate more on the front-row attack. Unless you are in a situation where you have one hitter and five diggers out there, then you might want to try it. In that situation, you are going to have kids hitting against three blockers all of the time if they are up against any knowledgeable coach on the other side of the court. I think that a lot of times, too, the back-row attack is overblown too much and overused at too young of an age. The kids just are not [ready]. Yes, they have to start learning it at some point, but especially at the high school level, that is not an easy thing to do.

CV: If a high school player has great topspin on a ball, does that increase the effectiveness of the back-row attack?

AB: Again, I think that is a key element to being successful—being able to hit the ball and hit it hard and with spin so the ball travels that distance and it is going to drop. A lot of times, an element that is missing with women athletes that I think is a real difference from, for instance, young boys (and even the boys who play baseball vs. the boys who do not play baseball) is the ability to determine the spin of the ball. An athlete who plays baseball is taught to watch the pitcher and watch the ball. They understand the movement of the ball and what spin does to it. I do not think that young girls pick that up and understand that a ball coming to them, whether it is a knuckle ball or whether it is a topspin ball, is not the same. [For a long time, girls did not learn to read that ball at a young age like a boy playing baseball would. Now, I guess young girls playing softball may pick that up, yet that ball is coming underhand and it is a little bit different than the boys who are throwing it overhand. [Perhaps teaching

Technique Points in the Back-Row Attack
•Point of take-off
•Angle of approach
•Double arm swing
•Contact just in front of the body
•Contact at top of jump
•Full arm swing follow-through
•Slight forward travel
•Wrist snap
•Arch of back
•Steering ball with wrist
•Full arm extension
•Balanced landing

(Gordon, *Coaching Volleyball*, August/September 1988, 26.)

According to Banachowski, in the back-row attack, a player cannot hit the ball straight down because there is 6 to 8 feet the ball has to travel before it crosses the net.

I think another thing to take into consideration is to make players realize that when they are hitting in the back row, every set is not going to be perfect. They are not going to be able to put every ball away, so they may want to think about where they can hit the ball to get themselves out of trouble.

young girls to recognize the difference in ball spin should be done early in their careers.]

I think another thing to take into consideration is to make players realize that when they are hitting in the back row, every set is not going to be perfect. They are not going to be able to put every ball away, so they may want to think about where they can hit the ball to get themselves out of trouble. Most kids will hit the ball to the center of the court because they think that is the safest place to be hitting the ball; they have less room to make an error. If they ever took any of their math principles that they learned in a geometry class about angles and hypotenuse, they would realize the longest distance on the court is the opposite corner. Even down the line is longer than right to the middle. The players must figure out where they are attacking. [Teach the players to] hit it to either corner. If they are attacking on the right side, hit the ball to the cross-court corner. They have a lot more court to hit to and a lot less angle to worry about. The diggers will never stay on the back row and dig that ball — they will all creep into the middle of the court because they see the boys hit the ball straight down and they think that is what the girls are going to do, too, and that is not always what happens. I think a really smart back-row attacker learns to work the court rather than just attacking the ball. That is something that coaches can work on with the younger kids. Learn to work the court and not just work at hitting the ball hard. Players need to make sure that they can send the ball to certain areas that they want to attack. If I were setting up drills with the young kids, that would be one thing that I would teach them to do.

One thing that we have done in the past couple of years in our practice is to lay a tape across the last 5 feet of the court. As a warm-up drill and a hitting and blocking drill, we will set 4s and 5s and go until we get a +15 on that back line. If the players hit the ball in front of that line, it counts as nothing; if they hit it out-of-bounds, we minus them. If they hit it way long, we will minus them, also. But if they hit it just a little long, we will not minus them so that they learn to work in that particular area. We do the drill with a block and without a block so that they get an idea of having one there. You can do that same sort of thing with the back row just by putting the tape back there or laying the tape in an area and have the players learn to hit the ball there.

CV: How much of a part does the back-row attack play in your offense in terms of percentage? What do you see as a normal percentage?

AB: The surprising thing was that in the 1992 season, our efficiency out of the back row was not very good, but our kill percentage was. The back-row attack makes up about seven to eight percent of our offense, while I imagine the national team is up around 10 percent. It was a little disheartening that we did not have a better back-row efficiency, yet we did not care because our kill percentage was still pretty good. And, we are always hoping that those kills would come at the right time.

Andy Banachowski is the head women's volleyball coach at UCLA.

Photo: Scott Quintard, ASUCLA

While hitting from the back row, players must realize that not every set is going to be perfect; as a result, placement of the ball on the opponent's court is paramount.

Setter and Quick Hitter Efficiency

Setter and Quick Hitter Efficiency

MARK PAVLIK

The relationship between the quick hitter and the setter is one in which both players not only rely upon, but also enhance, the other's performance. Therefore, it is crucial to create situations in practice where the quick hitter and setter can learn how each other will react. The performance of the quick hitter and the setter become critical to the execution of the offense if and only if a team has reached a level of passing efficiency enabling an up-tempo multiple attack offense to be run.

SIDEOUT OPPORTUNITIES

An attacker will have the opportunity to swing at a ball in two situations: the sideout offense and in transition. The sideout offense holds great importance because the opponent simply cannot score if the ball is put away off the first swing. This importance is magnified in rally score games. The transition swing can result in a point scoring opportunity or another sideout opportunity, but generally is less patterned and more predictable than the first swing sideout offense. Many times, transition offense appears to be an exercise in chaos with a poorly controlled first contact, attackers scrambling to find the ball visually and the setter penetrating at any angle. Since the setter is in motion, the quick hitter may be unsure of a take-off point for an efficient swing at a set. Moreover, if the setter is not aware of the quick hitter's approach is it any surprise the ball usually goes high and outside? The predictability of the transition offense is centered around the apparent chaotic reaction of the blockers trying to become attackers.

Effective transition and sideout multiple offense requires attackers visually to find and react to the first contact, the setter getting to the ball under control and the quick attacker being in the air as a target when the setter has the ball. It also requires an extremely tenacious attitude and an unwavering work ethic on the part of the quick hitter. The responsibility with that position is to be in the air when the setter has the ball every time the ball crosses the net.

Much like the defensive axiom of "no judgment being made as to whether or not a ball is playable until maximum effort to play the ball is exerted," the quick hitter has no judgment to make except how to get in the air when the setter has the ball—no matter the result of the first contact. The quick hitter must transition off the net after blocking. It helps to turn toward the area which the ball is directed while landing on the opposite foot and running in search of the ball. The quick hitter must realize, at times, the classical approach may not be effective due to time and distance factors, so improvisation must be encouraged. Great athletes always find ways to get their bodies in position to execute a skill, so demand the quick hitter be in the air every time the setter has the ball. This does not mean the quick hitters should consider themselves as "fakers." Every coach has seen a pass followed by a set outside and as the outside set is peaking the quick hitter has just jumped and executed a perfect armswing. This deceives no one and offensively covers nobody but the net tape. It is the setter's responsibility to decide if the quick hitter is the

According to Pavlik, the responsibility of the quick hitter is to be in the air when the setter has the ball every time the ball crosses the net.

Photo: Ball State University

Generally, I believe the setter should determine the team patterns (much as a carefully trained quarterback calls his own plays). While it is probably a good idea to allow communication between the attacker and the setter, ultimately the setter should be able to determine specific weaknesses in the opposition, react to the situation and call for an offensive pattern that takes advantage of the current offensive strengths and defensive weaknesses.

(Beal, Doug. (1987). Offensive combinations. *The AVCA Volleyball Handbook*. Indianapolis, IN: Masters Press, 150.)

Younger quick hitters and younger setters seem afflicted by a similar problem: standing and watching a teammate pass the ball, then attempting to initiate their own movement. Invariably, unless the pass is extremely high, the setter is late getting to the ball and the quick hitter is late, also.

best option for which to deal the ball. The quick hitter must always be in the air looking for the set, giving the setter that option and being prepared to do something with the ball but never ever being a "faker."

GETTING THE HITTER AND SETTER IN SYNC

It is important to get into the practice gym to get the setters and quick hitters working in unison. Begin by establishing where at the net the setter will penetrate. I prefer to have the setter penetrate to the right front corner then move to the pass at target. This enables the setter to view the entire court and have the weight forward when setting. This should also eliminate any backpedaling to balls passed to the extreme right of the court.

Secondly, insist the setter jumpset the ball at every opportunity. This promotes a quicker exchange from setter to hitter. Show where the ball is to be set when running any quick series (i.e. 31, 41, 51, 61, etc.). The preference is to set the ball anywhere from the midline of the setter's body to the left shoulder in relation to the net.

This motion is used when setting a ball to the outside. Also, it will force the quick hitter to jump, keeping the ball (and the setter) between him/her and the net. This gives the hitter a full armswing and follow-through without worry of raking the net and allows the hitter a wider visual perspective of the potential block being faced.

This take-off style can be altered if the pass pulls the setter off the net. The quick hitter may then be at a 45-degree angle from the setter and as far away from the setter as the ball is from the net with hips open to the setter. The hitter must still be in a position where the swing and follow-through will be unencumbered by the net. The setter will then "shoot" the ball in front of the hitter's shoulder closest to the net.

The second option is to have the quick hitter's take-off remain constant in relation to the setter, as described above. The view of the block and all hitting angles will not be affected; however, a flat shot will be required and can be extremely effective in this situation. Another benefit gained is not requiring the setter to change any mechanics in delivering this set. Again, encourage players to experiment with these options as often as possible. The one that becomes most effective will be that with which they become most confident.

As mentioned before, the quick hitter must visually find the ball as he/she is transitioning from the net. Younger quick hitters and younger setters seem afflicted by a similar problem: standing and watching a teammate pass the ball, then attempting to initiate their own movement. Invariably, unless the pass is extremely high, the setter is late getting to the ball and the quick hitter is late also.

Encourage the setter to release from defense immediately upon identifying that the ball will not be attacked into their defensive area of responsibility. With the quick hitter, emphasize a quick transition from the net, running with the head up and searching for the ball with a forward lean to the body. Their attention must be on the ball, not the setter. Too many times the opportunity for an effective transition swing is eliminated due to the quick hitter watching and literally arriving on the setter. Suggest that the quick hitter keep the ball outside and slightly in front of the right shoulder and follow it as if the ball has the hitter on a short leash. If the hitter is leaving the ground as the pass is falling to about head level, the timing should put them in the air as the setter has the ball.

To help the quick hitters and setters develop these parts of their game, devise a simple pass-set-quick hit drill. Initiate this drill by tossing a ball over the net to a passer who overheads the ball to the setter, who jump-sets the quick attack. This mirrors a free ball situation and allows the setter and quick hitter to follow the ball. (You may choose to have another setter be the passer.) Then run the same drill with the setter and quick hitter originating from their respective serve reception areas. You may find the players making small adjustments to their starting positions so they become more comfortable initiating their hitting lanes.

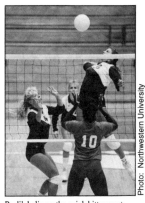

Pavlik believes the quick hitter must emphasize a quick transition from the net. The attention must be on the ball, not the setter.

The next step is to add a transition drill for the setters and hitters. Several options exist for this type of drill. One is to have a controlled hit off of a stand with the quick hitter attempting to block. The ball is passed to the setter for the transition quick set. Another option is to add one, two or even three possible front-row attackers, forcing the quick hitter to move to block then attack. The attackers can be asked to establish offensive coverage when hitting then move to their blocking responsibilities to try to stop the oncoming quick attack. The rally may be played out with the team of attackers only hitting to a specified area. It is important to have the setter penetrate from the back row and also block in these drills (if your setter is asked to block in competition) so they learn to get to the ball under control and jumpset in a myriad of situations.

Yet another drill series that involves a segment of the game is a one-on-one competition. The quick attacker is swinging at any quick series set against a commit blocker or a double block. The result of the swing can be in favor of the attacker (e.g. killer blockers' net violation) or of the blockers (e.g. stuff block, controlled block or hitting error). Immediately after the ball passes the block or is blocked the next ball is put in play in the blockers' side of the net forcing transition to occur on both sides of the net. These drills can be designed to have the quick hitter transition right-to-left or left-to-right both in attacking and blocking.

The next step is to move to a six-on-six situation where a kill resulting from a quick attack is weighted more heavily than any other kill or where the only front-row attack must be a quick series set; any other attack must be a back-row attack. Decide what your team must do to be successful with the quick attack and design your own unique drills to address those needs.

One extremely important concept needs to be discussed. Blocking schemes are becoming more and more sophisticated and the one-ball set off the setter is not as worrisome to the blocking team as in the past. The commit blocker just sets up near the setter and expects an approximately perpendicular approach by the quick hitter directly to the setter. The offensive advantage may not be that great even if the quick hitter is up on time. The advantage will be reclaimed if the commit block is not as solid or is reaching. The concept of making the blocker move by "chasing" the hitter is an important one.

For the quick attack to be effective, passing must be at an efficient level, the setter must consistently get to the ball and the quick hitter must always transition and be in the air when the setter has the ball.

In the men's game, quick hitters play higher above the net and "hang" longer than their female counterparts, appearing to "fly" past blockers. However, the slide set in the women's game can accomplish the same effect as a moving hitter passes through a stationary blocker's field of vision. In any quick attack drill, either for the sideout offense or in transition, work with the quick attackers to develop a more parallel approach to attack to "daylight" or simply between blockers.

As quick hitters and setters develop the necessary tenacity and intuitive communication, drills can be designed to promote tactical considerations of the quick attack. But, for the quick attack to be effective, passing must be at an efficient level, the setter must consistently get to the ball and the quick hitter must always transition and be in the air when the setter has the ball. The entire offense will rise to a higher level if these responsibilities are carried out every time the ball passes across the net.

Mark Pavlik is the head men's volleyball coach at Penn State University and is a USA Volleyball CAP Level II accredited coach.

One Leg Up on the Opposition

One Leg Up on the Opposition

"I was happy to see Petticord graduate so we would not have to see her flying back and pounding slides against us, but Cunningham is the best I have ever seen. How do you teach them to do it so well?" In recent years, I have heard this question more than once. The easy answer is that Lisa Petticord and Kelley Cunningham, both West Coast Conference players of the year and U.S. Olympic Festival medalists, are tremendous, hardworking athletes who naturally picked up the slide due to their strong backgrounds in basketball. The truth is, however, that I have developed some specific guidelines for teaching this skill based on several years of experimentation and careful observation of these two great Gonzaga slide attackers in action.

According to Madden, while the one-leg attack has become prevalent, there has been little written on the appropriate mechanics and concepts involved in maximizing its potential.

While the one-leg attack has become prevalent in the world of women's volleyball and is slowly making its way into the men's game, there has been little written on the appropriate mechanics and concepts involved in maximizing its potential. As a start, this discussion will center on teaching the slide as an individual skill.

For purposes of simplifying references, any attack executed from a one-leg take off is referred to as a "slide" herein. Correspondingly, any attack executed from a two-leg take off is referred to as "traditional." While most coaches have employed the back slide, where the athlete is moving in the same direction as the ball, this discussion includes the rare front slide, where the athlete is moving toward a low, lob set. The principles of execution are essentially the same, though some unique elements of the front slide will also be discussed.

FUNDAMENTAL GUIDELINES FOR SLIDE ATTACKS

There are five guidelines that are fundamental to all slide attacks and which vary from technique for traditional attacks. These should be clearly explained and demonstrated to athletes early in the learning process.

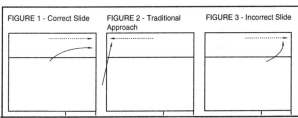

•Guideline 1—The attacker should be moving parallel to the flight of the set at takeoff. In the case of a perfect pass, this means that the player is running parallel to the net as she plants her final step and jumps (Figure 1). This varies significantly from the traditional approach, which takes the athlete toward the net at a 60 percent angle (Figure 2). In order to achieve this parallel position, the attacker must bend her approach starting toward the net, then curving toward the sideline. Many athletes have a natural urge to bend in the opposite direction, starting toward the sideline, then curving toward the net (Figure 3). This negates their ability to catch up with the ball and generate power through body turn as explained in guidelines three and four.

•Guideline 2—The athlete should accelerate into and through the takeoff. Unlike traditional approaches which emphasize transferring forward speed into upward force through a braking concept, a slide approach involves no effort to stop forward movement. The player simply lifts while flying forward, much like a long-jumper.

•Guideline 3—The attacker should catch up with the ball. Unlike a traditional approach, where the athlete intercepts the ball from an intersecting approach pattern, on a slide it is important that the player generate enough acceleration on her approach that she is moving faster than the set and can fly to catch it along her parallel line. This means that the takeoff point should be at least 1 meter from the anticipated point of attack with the exact distance being dependent upon the flight range of the individual athlete (Figure 4).

•Guideline 4—The attacker should rotate her body into the swing as she is jumping and flying to the ball.

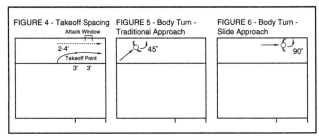

While a traditional approach allows approximately 45 degrees of body turn initiated at the hip to generate power (Figure 5), the slide allows 90 degrees of turn initiated with a knee and hip drive, which should add a significant amount of power to the culminating armswing (Figure 6).

•Guideline 5—The attacker should open a window of attack opportunity that is at least 2 feet wide and preferably a full meter (one attack zone in a nine-zone system). As the ball enters the window, the attacker wants to have the ability to reach it simultaneously with a solid swing. As the

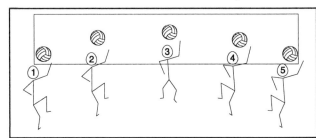

FIGURE 7

ball floats through the window, the player, who is traveling faster than the ball, wants to drift past it and have the ability to attack it at any given point in the window (Figure 7). This wide window effect is the major advantage of the slide over traditional attacks: Rather than presenting one attack point on which the block can set itself, the slide opens a range of attack that clearly negates the effectiveness of a narrow single block and even diminishes the value of a solid double block. While a traditional attack requires that the hitter cut the ball around the block in one direction or the other with an arm turn and/or body tuck, a slide attack allows the athlete to beat the block by simply attacking the ball early in the window before it reaches the block, waiting a fraction of a second until the athlete and the ball float to a point in the window where a seam presents itself, or waiting another smidgen until the athlete and the ball reach the end of the window past the block. To maximize the window, it is essential that the athlete perfect both timing and spacing.

TIME AND SPACE CONCEPTS

One of the most crucial understandings that a coach and player must have in order to develop great attacking abilities is that time and space are two distinct variables. The importance of this recognition is accentuated in the case of slide attacking. All too often, a coach addresses or an attacker adjusts temporal and spatial variables as though they are one and the same. For example, a player may constantly run under the ball on a traditional approach and the coach says, "You are in early" or the player thinks that he/she needs to wait in order to avoid going too far. To correct what is clearly a spacing problem, the player then adjusts his/her timing by delaying the start of the approach, which does cause him/her to stay further behind the ball because he/she is rushed and chops steps to try to get up on time. The correct feedback for this prevalent problem is, "Your timing is perfect; adjust your spacing to take off further from the net and stay behind the ball."

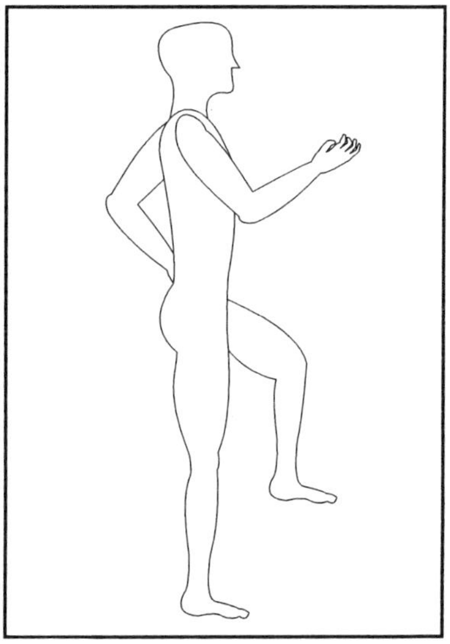

In the case of slide attacks, most players tend to make spacing mistakes that cause them to be ahead of the ball where they have to slow themselves down rather than accelerate to and through their takeoff. This common mistake essentially shuts the attack window to a narrow opening, which is easy for the block to read. Players also tend to take a parallel line too close to the line traveled by the ball, which limits the ability to generate power through body rotation and use their vision to see the block. In general, if proper spacing is strictly adhered to, timing problems can be easily solved.

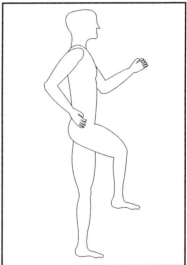

FIGURE 8 - Attacker's approach position at setter contact -- first tempo set timing

Proper spacing begins with the attacker approaching on a line parallel to the path of the set and 2-4 feet away from the ball. This allows room for the body to rotate on an axis at the nonhitting hand side of the body and for contact of the hitting hand with the ball to occur out in front of the body.

The most crucial element of spacing is that the takeoff foot plants 3-5 feet (1-1.5 zones in a nine-zone system) from the beginning of the attack window. This allows the athlete ample room to accelerate up to the ball as he/she rises on the jump. As the player rises, he/she is traveling faster than the ball, then usually naturally decelerates to a speed approximating that of the ball as he/she leaves the attack window (hopefully after launching the ball toward the opposition's floor).

Through years of observation and experimentation, we have developed some very clear-cut timing cues for slide attacks. These cues key on the setter's contact with the ball and may need to be adjusted slightly based on the speed of the setter's release and the speed of the individual attacker, but they seem to remain fairly consistent. For a first-tempo set (a ball which peaks 1-2 feet above the net tape), the hitter should be crossing his/her left foot past the right leg going into the last approach step as the ball touches the setter's hands (Figure 8). For a second-tempo set (a ball which peaks 3-4 feet above the net tape), the hitter should be crossing his/her right foot past the left leg going into the second to the last step of the

FIGURE 9 - Attacker's approach position at setter contact -- first tempo set timing approach (Figure 9). We do not plan to hit third-tempo sets from one leg, as the downward trajectory of the ball negates the window concept discussed earlier.

The key to training time and space for slide attacks is to get the athlete to space so that he/she has to catch up with the ball and time an accelerating approach so that he/she does catch up to it. It is essential that the coach and the athlete learn to distinguish between being too far and being early as well as not being far enough and being late. It is best to check athletes' perspectives by asking them whether their problem is one of timing or spacing after each failed connection. It is essential that they learn to distinguish the actual cause of the breakdown on their own.

DEALING WITH PASSING VARIABLES

While effective slide attacking demands accurate passing with balls targeted to a constant zone at the net, it is possible to train hitters to adjust to out-of-system passes effectively and still run the slide.

The first adjustment to train is what the hitter should do when the setter is pulled off the net by the pass. The key here is that the slide approach is parallel to the path of the ball, not parallel to the net. Consequently, the hitter should move off the net further than the setter is pulled and start the approach run from there (Figure 10). This allows him/her to

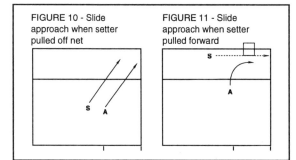

FIGURE 10 - Slide approach when setter pulled off net

FIGURE 11 - Slide approach when setter pulled forward

time and space the same as always relative to the ball, which should assure a good swing. The biggest sacrifice is that the hitter cannot rotate the body as much into the shot because he/she is already facing the net to some degree; attack power is likely to decrease. A second limitation is that the distance of the ball from the net early in the window restricts the attacker's ability to terminate the ball by hitting it straight down.

In general, the attack will still work if the set and approach move toward the net at an angle no greater than 45 degrees. If the setter's position dictates a sharper angle, then the hitter should audible to a zone further away from the setter or the setter should feed a different attack option.

The second adjustment to train is what the attacker should do when the setter is pulled forward along the net and the set is designated to go to a zone rather than move with the setter. If the setter is so far forward that the ball will be traveling more than 10 feet, it is probably impossible for the hitter to stay behind the ball the entire time and catch up to it. In this case, the hitter should be instructed to pull off the net to the 3-meter line at a point approximately 6 feet to the left of the takeoff point relative to the net. Then, as the ball is set, the player should be moving forward with normal timing and bending the approach to pull in alongside the passing ball; it will begin to decelerate as the athlete accelerates into the final step, allowing him/her to catch up to it in the end (Figure 11). This movement is similar to a car merging into high-speed traffic by making a gradual right curve and accelerating in a parallel lane where the passing traffic initially is moving faster; eventually, it can build speed to then catch up to that traffic.

The final adjustment to train is what the hitter should do when the setter is pushed back into the attack zone so that the set will go virtually straight up and down. In this case, the attacker should simply maintain the same timing and spacing as always relative to the ball at its attackable point and anticipate that the block will be better able to set up on the ball, necessitating sharper attack angles or an offspeed shot. While the ball must be attacked from the middle of the window, the attacker can use his/her flying body position to attack the ball early as she enters the window or late as he/she exits to create angles around the block.

Madden believes that in training slide attackers, it is important to emphasize that they must trust their setter to make the perfect set.

DEALING WITH SETTING VARIABLES

Outstanding slide attackers will be able to deal with a variety of setting mistakes without committing attack errors. An advantage of slide attacks is that inaccurate sets should be less costly than in the case of traditional quicksets if the attacker is maintaining proper spacing and timing. This is true because the ball, regardless of the setting miscue involved, will always be out in front of the attacker where he/she can clearly see it and make last-second adjustments as he/she reaches it.

In the case of a low set, the attacker will want to contact the ball early in the window with a push shot into or around the block or a quick chip shot back toward the center of the opposition's court. It is crucial that the hitter's line of approach is far enough from the line of the set to allow room to reach out and accomplish these shots. In the case of a high set, the attacker will want to decelerate slightly in the last step of the approach in order to delay takeoff from the ground and allow the ball to drop back down to attackable height. The hitter should avoid the temptation to try to bury this ball, as the jump and reach will have been diminished by the deceleration and the risk of taping the shot becomes significant.

If the setter does not push the set far enough, the attacker should try to jump more upward as he/she plants so that he/she adjusts the window back to that of the ball. If the setter pushes the set too far out, the attacker should jump as far as possible without regard for getting high, still catching up to the ball and at least wristing it into play.

When the set travels too tight to the net, the hitter should adjust the jump to sail toward the net and look for a tool or wipeshot opportunity. When the set goes too far off the net, the attacker should limit body rotation to keep the hitting shoulder further off the net and take a cross-body swing to create a high, flat shot to the deep corners of the opposition's court.

In training slide attackers, it is important to emphasize that they must trust their setter to make the perfect set. Anticipating bad sets leads to non-dynamic approaches, improper timing and spacing adjustments and other breakdowns, which destroy the effectiveness of the slide as a weapon. On the other hand, it is important to create bad set situations in training that force the attacker to make the adjustments outlined above at the last second and keep the ball in play. Over time, such adjustments will become second nature and often result in highly effective and unpredictable attacks that score. When a setter knows he/she can trust the slide attacker to bail him/her out, he/she is much more likely to dish the slide at any time.

The fundamental guidelines for slide attacking are essentially the same for front slides as back. The concept of catching up to the ball is lost because the hitter and ball are guaranteed to pas in flight, but the need for the hitter to accelerate and fly forward remains as the key to creating a wide attack window.

UNIQUE ASPECTS OF THE FRONT SLIDE

The slide gives the attacker an advantage over the block because it incorporates lateral motion along the net, which makes proper block placement very difficult. As originally conceptualized, the slide is a back attack where the ball and hitter are traveling in the same direction at slightly different speeds through an attack window. Most teams have limited their use of the slide to same-direction lateral movement. At Gonzaga, we have had a great deal of luck incorporating front slides where the ball and hitter are moving in exactly opposite directions. The original advantage of lateral motion still exists and the attack window actually becomes bigger in the case of front slides, though the difficulties of timing and spacing become greater.

The fundamental guidelines for slide attacking are essentially the same for front slides as back. The concept of catching up to the ball is lost because the hitter and ball are guaranteed to pass in flight, but the need for the hitter to accelerate and fly forward remains as the key to creating a wide attack window. The attack window remains in the same location relative to the attacker's takeoff point, but while the attacker is entering one side the ball is entering the other. Though the player can attack the ball at any point in the window because the player and ball pass each other more quickly, the time differential between early and late becomes minuscule. Consequently, the front slide requires a much faster read of the block and quicker armswing by the hitter. Front slides become problematic when the ball is traveling so fast that it does not hang in the window so the fast-flying hitter can turn and spank it, thus first-tempo sets can only be run a couple of zones away from the setter while second tempo sets, which travel more slowly, can be run several zones in front of the setter.

Because it is impossible for the attacker to follow a line parallel to the ball when the setter is off the net (this would require approaching from the other side of the net), the front slide attacker always takes an approach that parallels the net, regardless of where the pass pulls the setter. Because the setter is always visible out in front, there is also no need to adjust the approach for him/her being pulled forward or pushed backward. Thus, the approach for a front slide actually presents fewer adjustment problems than that for a back slide.

Adjusting to inaccurate sets is the same on a front slide as a back slide with these two exceptions: When the ball is set too far forward, the attacker should make the same adjustment as for a ball that is not set far enough on a back slide and when the ball is not set far enough forward, the attacker should make the same adjustment as for a ball that is set too far for a back slide.

SUMMARY

Running the slide does require great passing, excellent coordination between setter and attacker, quick and explosive athletes and extensive training time, but the rewards are huge. Any attacker who naturally jumps off of one leg and gets as high or higher than off of two will become a better weapon if trained to hit slides following the guidelines above.

Sean Madden is the head women's volleyball coach at Gonzaga University and is a USA Volleyball CAP Level III candidate.

The Right Side Attack

The Right Side Attack

JOEY VRAZEL

For the past several years, we have seen some of volleyball's most versatile and dynamic athletes play the right side position. Often referred to as the "weak side," the right side attack has increasingly become a major offensive focus, both at the international and collegiate level.

Team USA's Caren Kemner and Natalie Williams are two examples of how dominating a right side attacker can be. Both possess outstanding blocking, swing hitting and back-court attacking abilities, the latter becoming a more critical component in being successful at the international level. It is also common to see teams moving middle blockers to the right side to tap into their major blocking and quick hitting potential.

This article addresses many components with regard to the right side attack. Certain offensive and defensive advantages will be identified. Characteristics of a good right side hitter will be pointed out, as well as training cues and technique.

Offensively, if the right side hitter is able to hit a slide and quick attacks, especially in transition, the offensive options are unlimited.

ADVANTAGES OF THE RIGHT SIDE ATTACK

There are many advantages to implementing the right side attack. First, a right side attack is difficult to defend because most defensive schemes are geared to expect a majority of attacks to come from the left side. By using your right side offense, you create a situation where the opposing setter now becomes a primary digger, the opposing left side hitter becomes a major blocker and the opponent's help blocking in the middle becomes less effective. It also requires the opposing team to honor all hitters instead of release blocking to the power side, especially if the right side is run quick.

Offensively, if the right side hitter is able to hit a slide and quick attacks, especially in transition, the offensive options are unlimited. In a system which maximizes the middle attack, a quick first- or second-tempo set to the right side is a very effective choice, especially with a hitter who can effectively hit both line and angle.

Training a right side player also includes setter training and can involve teaching that hitter to run the middle attack offense. This option can provide your offense with even more weapons. In all cases, a great deal of training and considerable repetition will be required.

Training a right side player also includes setter training and can involve teaching that hitter to run the middle attack offense. This option can provide your offense with even more weapons. In all cases, a great deal of training and considerable repetition will be required.

IDENTIFYING THE RIGHT SIDE ATTACKER

The first step in training the right side player is to identify an athlete on your team with the necessary physical skills. The following is a brief checklist when looking for that special player:
- whether left or right handed, lines the ball up well on hitting shoulder;
- capable of hitting both line and angle;
- good blocking ability;
- adequate setting ability;
- quick thinker;

40

An effective right side player must be able to hit both line and angle shots from a wide variety of approach angles.

Photo: Norm Schindler, ASUCLA

• possesses explosive movement;
• aggressive player who works to become attack available at all times; and
• capable of adjusting to varying passing alignments.

After you have selected your right side players, position specific training can now begin.

THE APPROACH

The approach is much like a middle blocker's in transition. A shortened, quick approach is preferred. At times, a two-step approach must be utilized in order to get in to hit quick. This applies to left handers as well as right handers, although lefties will back slightly outside of the court area for their approach.

ARMSWING & FOOTWORK

With regard to the approach, an effective right side player must be able to hit both line and angle shots from a wide variety of approach angles. Two components which impact this shot selection ability are the armswing (point of contact) and footwork.

In a hitting line, an influential right side player must be capable of letting the ball pass to the hitting shoulder if right-handed and to the opposite shoulder if left-handed.

The right side players and the setter must have a good working relationship. Being able to move quickly from defense to offense or vice versa and to communicate well is critical in order to run an efficient offense.

For optimal results, you want your right side players to position themselves on their approach to hit "all options." This is especially true if the set varies and travels inside or outside its anticipated flight. When this happens, the right side hitter must be able to react quickly with the first step to achieve that ideal "all option" position.

This is a difficult concept for beginning right-handed players to grasp. Most young hitters have trouble getting in good position and letting the ball cross their body to their hitting shoulder in order to hit a true line and end up hitting primarily angle/seam. Letting the ball cross over to that position between the head and hitting shoulder will allow a player to hit a true line shot.

It is important to note that unlike hitting on the left side, a right-handed player does not "open" the shoulders to the setter when hitting on the right side. Instead, the shoulders are parallel to the net during the approach; then, as they explode into their jump, the left shoulder "closes" to the net to allow for correct shoulder rotation. This must occur to hit either line or angle.

RELATIONSHIP WITH THE SETTER

The right side players and the setter must have a good working relationship. Being able to move quickly from defense to offense or vice versa and to communicate well is critical in order to run an efficient offense. Practice plans must incorporate these two positions working together in transition.

RELATIONSHIP WITH THE MIDDLE

The relationship between the middle and right side is important in establishing an effective transition offense. If the middle blocker is efficient and quick to call their attack, the right side can call options based on what the middle hitter runs. This transition between the middle and the right is something you must practice. Drills must be devised to establish the kind of working relationship you want to have between these two positions. This type of training is also crucial for the setter. It is very difficult to process verbal calls as quickly as they happen on the court. The setters can learn to process verbal calls quickly if they are able to practice them in a gamelike situation.

ESTABLISHING A RIGHT SIDE ATTACK

When creating a ride side attack, you can devise an offense that works to exploit opposing blockers and require them to make a decision to go with either the middle or the right side attack (but not to be able to get to both). You can choose to spread the offense (antennae to antennae) or to overload a zone. Several examples of right side-middle hitting combinations are illustrated in Figures 1 and 2.

Drills can be initiated at first by having the right side and middle hitter start at the net and come off for a free ball. The middle quickly gives a verbal call (based on the pass) and the right side makes a verbal call immediately afterwards. In all cases, calls must be made by both hitters before the setter contacts the ball. You can pre-establish set calls if desired:

• If the middle hitter (MH) calls a 3 (shoot), then the right side (RS) automatically calls a 5 or slide.

• If MH calls a 1, then RS runs an "X."

• If MH calls a slide, then RS hits a front 2.

You can let the hitters be free to call whatever they choose as long as they do not hit in the same zone. You can also establish a game plan beforehand either to spread the offense or overload a zone and have the hitters make the calls accordingly.

As your hitters become more comfortable and your setter begins to adapt to setting verbal calls, you can vary the drill by running it off of a controlled dig from either the left or right side. This will require both hitters getting in opti-

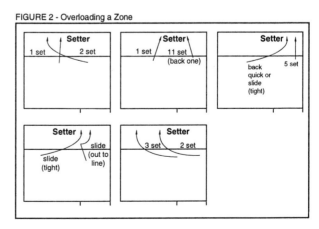

FIGURE 1 - Spreading the Offense

FIGURE 2 - Overloading a Zone

mal hitting position, coming off a block and being ready to "fire" forward. You will find they will be much more in tune and attack available when they are responsible for creating the play.

Inherent within the drills are bad passes and bad digs. Nevertheless, the middle hitter should still try to get attack available and the right side must continue to let the setter know what they are available to hit. Bad passes will, of course, simplify the offense; but the hitters must work to evaluate the passes quickly and make the appropriate call. This, too, will take time and mistakes will be made. The important thing for your setter to remember is that there is always an outlet on the left side if trouble arises. Coaches must work with their setter in learning to make the right choices and, in turn, not forcing a set. If the setter does not get in good position (to the net and stationary), it will be difficult for accurate sets and appropriate judgments to be made.

With time and practice, establishing an effective, attack available right side can give you tremendous flexibility and variety.

Establishing these options on the right side should give the hitters available shots to hit because the block will either be forming late or a one-on-one situation will be created. This is why it is so important for the hitter to be able to hit both line and angle and be able to take advantage of less-than-perfect blocking alignments. A late forming block is ideal to hit against because not only does it open up shots, but it can create havoc with the opposing team's back court. Because most hitters hit angle well, the opposing team's setter suddenly becomes a high percentage digger, forcing this player either to dig the first ball or hold the defensive position longer than normal. In the latter case, the opposing setter will have a difficult time getting to the net to run an offense.

SUMMARY

With time and practice, establishing an effective, attack available right side can give you tremendous flexibility and variety. Much is yet to be discussed about this position, especially with regard to the value of hitting out of the back court. Nonetheless, you will begin to notice what a great advantage it is to have a "power" hitter on the right side and will see that the right side position will play a deciding factor in many future matches.

Joey Vrazel is the head women's volleyball coach at Purdue University.

Splitting the Block

Splitting the Block

There are two major factors in running an offense that result in splitting or freezing the opponent's block. One is the offensive gameplan, which has two components. The first component employs "deceptive rotations." The second component includes the plays that are run from the deceptive rotations. The second major factor is the deception created by the setter. A setter who is very deceptive can make up for a weak gameplan. The converse is also true. A great gameplan can make up for a setter who is weak in deception skills. This article will examine deceptive rotations and then touch on plays that can be run out of these rotations.

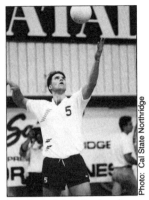

According to Redenbacher, deceptive rotations should be developed for a team when it is serving and when it is receiving serve.

DECEPTIVE ROTATIONS: A DEFINITION

Simply stated, a deceptive rotation is one that makes certain players appear to be in the front row when they are not and vice-versa. The major objective of deceptive rotations is to create confusion among the opponent's blockers before the ball is served. This confusion results in the other team blocking false hitters so your setter does not have to split the block by himself/herself.

Deceptive rotations have a tremendous advantage over the old hide-the-setter rotations where the setter had to step in front of the person with whom he/she overlapped just before the ball was served. With deceptive rotations, the setter (or hitter) need not go to his/her true position until after the ball is served. Therefore, the setter never gives away whether he/she is front or back row.

Even collegiate coaches and players are frequently unaware of the strategies available through deceptive rotations. Players often look at me with amazement when I describe these strategies. Suspicions are quickly dissipated when the players find out how well these deceptive tactics work.

DECEPTIVE ROTATIONS WHEN YOU ARE SERVING

Deceptive rotations should be developed for your team when it is serving and when it is receiving serve. When serving, deceptive rotations are most effective when making your setter, rather than a hitter, appear as if he/she is in the front row when he/she is actually in the back row and vice-versa. (For this article, I am assuming the use of the most commonly used offense, the 5-1. Deceptive rotations can be applied to the 6-2, sometimes referred to as the 6-0, and 4-2, although the objectives differ somewhat.)

Figures 1, 2 and 3 illustrate rotations when the setter's true position is in the front row. Note that the rotations make it appear that the setter is in the back row.

Figures 4, 5 and 6 illustrate some deceptive rotations when the setter is in the back row. Note that Figure 5 and Figure 6 make it appear that the setter is in the front row. Figure 4 merely tries to hide a hitter since the

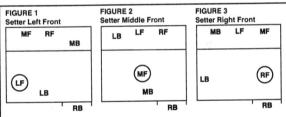

FIGURE 1
Setter Left Front

FIGURE 2
Setter Middle Front

FIGURE 3
Setter Right Front

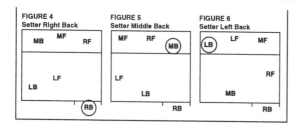

FIGURE 4
Setter Right Back

FIGURE 5
Setter Middle Back

FIGURE 6
Setter Left Back

setter is serving. Hiding a hitter in this instance is not particularly effective. Since the setter is serving, the other team is aware that there are three hitters. One might use a rotation like this, however, when attempting to convince the opponents to set away from the true left front (LF). Many setters call plays depending upon where the big blockers are on the other side of the net. Players will frequently cross the best hitter over against the weakest blocker. If LF is a weak blocker, Figure 4 just might keep opponents from purposely running a play at her.

Likewise, there is a distinct advantage in making the opposing team think your setter is in the back row (as in Figures 1, 2 and 3) as you serve. If the other team thinks that a big blocker is in a front-row position where the setter actually is, they may consciously set away from your setter. This benefit alone is worth implementing a deceptive rotation.

If your setter is in the back row, but appears to be in the front row, the other team should assign a blocker to this player if the ball is passed anywhere near the net. This means that a hitter is open somewhere. If the setter is in the front row, but the blockers believe he/she is a back-row player, no blocker will be assigned to her and the time is ripe for an attack by the setter.

There is a distinct advantage in making the opposing team think your setter is in the back row as you serve. If the other team thinks that a big blocker is in a front-row position where the setter actually is, they may consciously set away from your setter. This benefit alone is worth implementing a deceptive rotation.

Do not assume that the rotations illustrated here are all the deceptive rotations available. With a little imagination, you will come up with many more, but these are basic examples that can be employed by nearly any team.

QUALIFICATIONS

Some qualifications about deceptive rotations are in order. First, if no one in your league pays attention to where your setter or hitters are, you may not want to take the time to develop such strategies unless you expect to meet sophisticated teams in the playoffs, tournaments, etc.

Second, some will claim that the moment the players run to their true positions following the serve, the illusion is over. In all the years of running a deceptive rotation on our serve, I can only recall one team that noticed the switch during the play. I suspect that as volleyball becomes more sophisticated, teams will someday routinely look for such stratagems. Nevertheless, it is still exceedingly difficult to adjust in mid-play.

Sometimes the other team will cry, "Back-row blocker or attacker" after the play because they thought the setter or hitter was in the back row. This brings me to my next caution: warn the officials. Show them before the match the subtleties of your rotations. Referees are not particularly used to seeing rotations like this, even with collegiate play.

With the referees on notice, your players must watch zealously for overlap. For instance, in Figure 1, the most likely overlap would come from the MB being in front of the MF. Usually, you will want the person who is "out of position" to be primarily responsible for preventing overlap. It is MB's primary responsibility to be sure that he/she is behind MF. Another common source of overlap is LF being in back of LB or overlapping side to side with MF. Looking at each of the figures, you can determine where there is danger of overlap and which player is assigned the primary responsibility of preventing this violation. Sometimes the danger of overlap comes from side to side, sometimes front to back, sometimes both.

Coaches must be certain that their players will automatically go to their "false" positions in the deceptive rotation before the ball is served. Any hesitation or sudden adjustment in position will be a clue to the other team that something is up. You can, however, purposely use a sudden adjustment to fool the other side when you are actually playing it straight. Be careful, however, of overloading your players with too much detail. The key is practice and a keen awareness by each player of position on the court.

Jump setting is a skill in which every setter should be proficient. Jump setting not only helps to freeze a blocker, but aids the setter who attacks.

At the beginning of the game it is usually best to have your setter start at MB. This will momentarily keep the opposing team guessing where your setter really is in the rotation. Obviously, if you use your setter as the first server, the other team will figure out very quickly where his/her position is in the rotation.

Whatever you do, the prime consideration is to keep the other team guessing. If they have figured out what is going on, change things. Go back to a normal rotation, implement a completely different deceptive rotation or start your setter somewhere other than MB.

Also, where you start your setter has to be determined in light of other factors, such as 1) which player has the best serve 2) does having the setter in the front row too soon weaken the team, just to name a few.

THE SETTER AS ATTACKER WITHIN DECEPTIVE ROTATIONS

The setter attacking the second ball deserves special mention when discussing deceptive rotations and the ability to split the block.

There is no better way to freeze a blocker than if the opponents know that the setter, when in the front row, will attack the ball on the second contact. Jump setting is a skill in which every setter should be proficient. Jump setting not only helps to freeze a blocker, but aids the setter who attacks. The attack, however, need not necessarily be a hard-driven hit. A well-placed, deceptive dump will often be more effective. Coaches can help the setter by observing where the setter should dump the ball. One caution, though: be careful of dumping blindly, such as behind one's head, unless you are certain that there is not a blocker waiting. The setter needs to know where the blocker is and then quickly direct it past the block to the open floor.

Hitters and coaches alike tend to shudder when their setters put the ball over on the second hit. They get frustrated if the ball is picked up. The feeling is that if the setter had only set the ball, the hitter would have

According to Brassey-Iversen (1995), the setter can be an expert at deception.

"We like to run a lot of Xs. On occasion, we will tell our setter at the very beginning of the game to run the second option right away. Usually, that play will get blocked. They look at the bench and say, Good. That is perfect." Now our middle hitter is wide open. The next time we run the X they will wait for the second hitter."

(Brassey-Iversen, Laurel and Lorne Sawula. In-season performance evaluation of setters. *Critical Thinking on Setter Development*, 1995, 139.)

put it away. This is not necessarily so. A good hitter will hit somewhere in the neighborhood of .250 to .350. It is not all that uncommon to find a setter who can produce a hitting percentage of .300 with his/her dumps. A big reason for this is that a setter who dumps for accuracy rather than swinging will rarely blow the ball out, into the net or into the block. Remember, the setter usually has just one blocker on him/her and the defense is frequently out of position on the second attack. Just because the setter is not crushing the ball is no reason to restrict her attacks. Many high school teams are plagued by passing that is too close to the net. A setter who can attack effectively from the front row will be a big plus for such a team.

The ultimate goal, however, is to get the ball to the big hitters one-on-one with the blockers. If a setter is successful with her attacks, the opponent will eventually get the message and attempt to compensate by over-committing defensively, committing one blocker exclusively to the setter, and, possibly, double blocking the setter. When this finally occurs, the setter needs to start feeding the ball more and more to the hitters. The splits in the block will be most gratifying.

Gary Redenbacher is the former women's coach at Fresno State (Fresno, Calif.), and is currently an attorney in Santa Cruz, Calif.

Section III: The Block

The Evaluation of Blocking

The Evaluation of Blocking

JIM COLEMAN

About 13 years ago, I wrote an article titled "Option Blocking" (Coleman and Ford, 1983). In the article, I attempted to set forward a thought process upon which individual and team defense can be based. I have seen many rewritings of this article, but somehow, the thought processes appear to stray from my original intent.

On numerous occasions, I have presented the statistical results from my masters and doctoral research (Coleman, 1975) relating to the use of statistical systems in volleyball. Similarly, I have seen many rewritings with the scientific thought processes somewhat diminished from the original research findings.

Until recently, there has been little in the way of new or creative ideas in regard to blocking evaluation. This seems unfortunate since our statistical studies have always rated blocking as the first or the second determinant of success in winning volleyball matches. Attacking is the other major determinant and our attacking statistics have been well validated and documented. The lack of blocking studies is probably a strong indication that there is very little research related to volleyball coming out of our educational institutions. In the rush to recruit and to win matches, we have probably forgotten to ask, "Why are we doing this?" or "How can we do it better?"

With that as a backdrop, the best available research in this area includes four scientific studies of blocking (Coleman, 1975; Larsen, 1975; Schall; Eom and Schutz, 1992). The blocking statistics collected today are the following:
- stuff blocks
- assisted stuff blocks
- control blocks
- forced blocks.

According to Coleman, blocking is statistically the first or second determinant of success in volleyball.

ASSISTED STUFF BLOCKS

There are minor variations in the definitions and systems used by the NCAA and the USA national volleyball teams concerning stuff blocks and assisted stuff blocks. A "control block" is one in which the blocking team controls the ball well enough that it may mount an effective counter-attack after the block. The "forced block" is one in which the attacker hits the ball either into the net or out-of-bounds. This attacking error is supposedly forced by the intimidation of the block, thus the block is given some credit for the action. Research has shown a high correlation between the number of stuff blocks and the number of forced blocks; therefore, the category seems to be a valid one (Coleman, 1975; Larsen, 1975). Although these commonly kept statistics may be of some value to the coach, their true indication of blocking ability seems to be somewhat suspect. In my opinion, it is only the systems which keep data on all blocks which have a chance to be true indicators of blocking effectiveness.

Table 1

Blocking Evaluations and Definitions (Including numerical evaluation)

0	Kill by the attacker or blocker error
1	Ball blocked but attacking team receives a "free ball" from the block or defense
2	Ball in play to either side but no real advantage to either side
3	Ball controlled so that the defensive team has the option of a multiple counter attack 3
5	Block kill or attack error

*It should be noted that even though this is called a blocking statistical system, the fact is that often times, the success is related to the ability of the defenders playing behind or alongside the block.

Coleman devised a system to determine the "percent good" -- the percentage of times that a blocker jumps that something good happens for the team.

While accompanying the USA men's team on a trip to Cuba in March 1991, I documented scientific blocking statistics based on the definitions and numerical evaluations set forth in my doctoral research (see Table 1).

From these numerical evaluations given as the result of each block, individual and team blocking scores could be calculated. For instance, a goal of 1.75 was quite normal for the USA men's team blockers. Typically, I have kept the blocking evaluations separately for one, two or three blockers participating in the block.

Knowing how to combine the blocking results of solo versus combination blocks was always a problem which has not been investigated. My best guess was that a solo blocker receives full credit. If there were two blockers, each blocker received "half credit." Thus the two blockers, combined, received the "full credit." This would also hold true for three blockers

To compound the situation, the statistics were confusing because of various subcategories composing the various major categories, as listed in Table 2.

With this data in hand, USA Men's National Team Head Coach Fred Sturm began asking the types of questions which stimulate new thoughts and creative ideas. It was clear, after numerous hours of conversation, the problems we were facing appeared to be two-fold:

1) He was not familiar with the blocking average which I reported to him. He really had no experience upon which to base judgments. Although the numbers meant something to me, they meant nothing to him and he was the important person in the process of interpretation.

2) He wanted to know too much detail. I had to discern the most important information that he wanted and simplify it into terms which he could interpret.

My first attempt seemed simple enough. I defined a term which I call "percent good" — what is the percentage of times that a blocker jumps that something good happens for our team?

Using the five numerical evaluations of various blocking results (see Table 1), I calculated the percent good by combining the numbers of events in categories 2, 3 and 5, then dividing by the total number of blocking attempts (see equation to the left).

Table 2

Major Categories for Blocking (Including various subcategories)
Major Category 1 Kill by attacker or blocker error Subcategories a. No touch by block (No T) b. Touch by blocker receiving the score (TB) c. Touch by other blocker in a cooperative block (TOB) **Major Category II** Block kill or hitter error Subcategories a. Hitter error (ERR) b. Stuff by blocker receiving the score (STUF) c. Block by other blocker in a cooperative block or commonly called an "assist block" (ASST)

$$\text{percent good} = \frac{\text{category } (5 + 3 + 2) \times 100}{\text{total attempts}}$$

It seems quite reasonable to me that we will quickly learn to interpret these simple percentages. If percent good is 15 percent, the blocker is weak. If percent good is 50 percent, the blocker is phenomenal. Most blockers will fit somewhere in between.

Before this new system could even be evaluated, Sturm asked, "Why can't you just tell me the spiking efficiency of the attackers against each blocker?" I replied that, in fact, I could. It is simple!

The most important implication of his question was that we are already thinking in terms of spiking efficiencies. We already understand that evaluation process. Spiking efficiency was defined in 1955 and is the most accepted and widely used spiking term today (Coleman, 1972) as illustrated in Table 3.

To determine the spiking efficiency against a specific blocker, it is possible to convert the blocking system from my doctoral studies to the desired efficiency using the following formula:

$$\text{spiker efficiency vs. a blocker} = \frac{(\text{\# blocking 0's}) - (\text{\# blocking 5's}) \times 100}{\text{total blocking attempts}}$$

If spiking efficiencies against a blocker were the only blocking statistics to be kept, the tabulation system could be simplified to a system similar to that of spiking: the plus, zero, minus system. The coach/statistician must only be careful to remember whether the "plus" is a kill for the attacker or a kill for the blocker — just a simple but confusing bookkeeping problem.

The new system is being tested by both the men's and women's national teams. I am certain that the system will undergo many variations and changes. Testing is necessary. This system does seem to answer many of the problems associated with other blocking evaluations. It is simple, inclusive of all block attempts and understandable, since it uses the same system of evaluation that our current spiking system uses.

Table 3

I. Kill Percentage (*)

$$\text{Kill \%} = \frac{\text{Number of Kills} \times 100}{\text{Total attack attempts}}$$

II. Spiking Efficiency (*)

$$\text{Spiking Efficiency} = \frac{\text{Number of (kill - errors**)} \times 100}{\text{Total attack attempts}}$$

(*) It is common to leave these as the decimal equivalents and not convert them to percentages as they were defined originally.

(**) Errors = attack errors plus balls stuffed by blocker.

THOUGHTS FOR THE FUTURE

This blocking evaluation system needs to be tested and modified to meet the requirements of various coaches and teams; it also needs to be correlated to the probability of winning. Since spiking is currently being evaluated by our national teams in three categories before the values are totaled, blocking should probably be evaluated in the same manner. These categories include attack from serve reception; transition after serve reception, for sideouts; and transition for points. Finally, the blocking system needs to be related for a specific attacker against a specific blocker or group of blockers.

SUMMARY: TWO NEW SYSTEMS OF BLOCKING

In this article, two new systems of blocking evaluation have been presented. It is imperative that new questions are asked to further refine either or both of these systems. In addition, to determine the usefulness of the systems in its gross form, the system's subcategories need to be studied in subcategories within the context of the major categories.

REFERENCES

Coleman, Jim and T. Ford. Option blocking. *Journal of the National Volleyball Coaches Assn.,* IV, 2, May 1983, pp 3-12.

Coleman, Jim. A satistical evaluation of selected volleyball techniques at the 1974 World Volleyball Championships. Unpublished dissertation, Brigham Young University, 1975.

Coleman, Jim. The relationship between serving, passing, setting, attacking and winning in men's volleyball. Unpublished thesis, George Williams College, 1975.

Schall, Rod. Sportistics, Graceland College, Lamoni, IA.

Larsen, Ronald B. A statistical charting system for spike defense in men's international volleyball. Unpublished thesis, Brigham Young University, August 1975.

Coleman Jim. Report to the 1972 symposium on volleyball statistics. Verbal report, George Williams College, June 17, 1972.

Jim Coleman is the director of the National Volleyball Teams Training Center in San Diego, Calif., and is a member of the USA Volleyball CAP Cadre.

USA NATIONAL TEAM BLOCKING STATISTICS

USA vs._____

Tournament _____

NAME	# B L K	GAME ONE					GAME TWO					GAME THREE					GAME FOUR					GAME FIVE				
		0	1	2	3	5	0	1	2	3	5	0	1	2	3	5	0	1	2	3	5	0	1	2	3	5
	3																									
	2																									
	1																									
	3																									
	2																									
	1																									
	3																									
	2																									
	1																									
	3																									
	2																									
	1																									
	3																									
	2																									
	1																									
	3																									
	2																									
	1																									
	3																									
	2																									
	1																									
	3																									
	2																									
	1																									
	3																									
	2																									
	1																									
	3																									
	2																									
	1																									
	3																									
	2																									
	1																									
	3																									
	2																									
	1																									

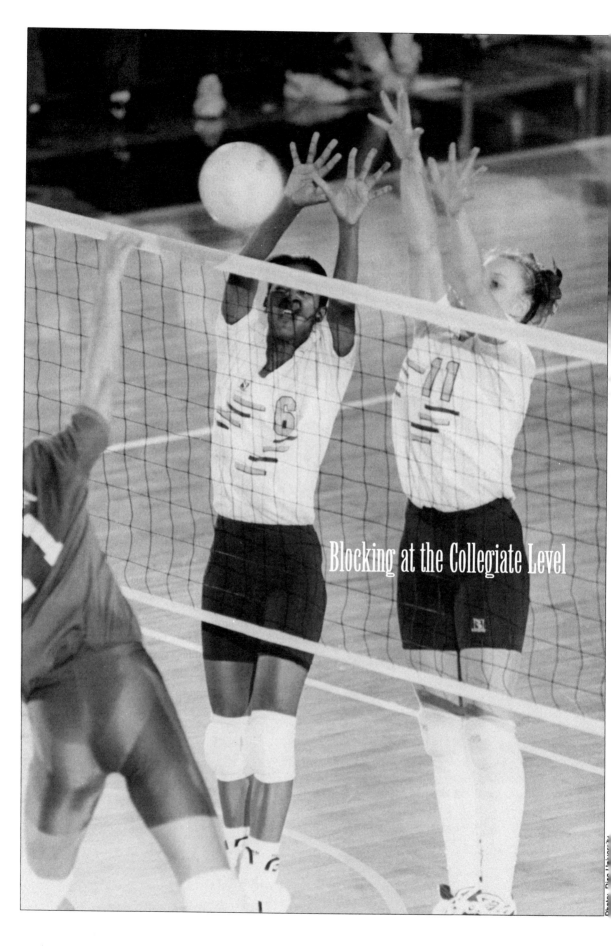

Blocking at the Collegiate Level

Blocking is an aggressive skill made better through confidence. To capitalize on this concept, a coach must design drills geared toward making players more confident, aggressive individuals.

BASIC PHILOSOPHIES

The best blockers are not necessarily the biggest players or the best jumpers. The qualities that great blockers possess are intensity, great vision, anticipation and, most of all, confidence in this particular skill.

Confidence, for some people, is an innate quality. For others, it must be nurtured. As a coach, you can design drills that not only improve skills but also build confidence, which we know is a desirable characteristic of successful athletes. Drills can be created, especially in the skill of blocking, that offer immediate success. Success equals confidence. Once the players have success they begin to think of themselves as better blockers.

Giovanazzi believes positive feedback builds better blockers.

It is important that during these training sessions you keep the feedback positive and aggressive. Phrases like "Grab the ball" and "Get the ball on their side" have a mental image of intensity and determination.

Like defense or coverage, I think the best blockers are the most reactive, assertive players on the court. It is a skill that is not based on technique but on attitude. Nonetheless, there are techniques that really enhance the skill. Like any other skill in this game, repetition is a vital component of development. The beauty of blocking is that in 10-15 minutes a day practicing blocking with your athletes, you will have immediate success. What that translates into is points for your team.

BLOCKING PROGRESSION

The progression that seems to be most useful begins with a coach standing on a box or stand 2-3 feet off the net. Individually, the players come from in front of the coach on the other side of the net and do a block jump, placing both hands around the ball that the coach is holding at the top of the net. This gets the athlete used to surrounding the ball. The arms of the blocker slide over the net.

The next step is to back the coach off the net to 3 or 4 feet. Using a controlled, low toss, the coach should attack the ball into the blocker's hands. The blocker must jump and time the ball the coach tosses and attacks. The immediate feedback is that if the blocker is not over the net, the ball will be blocked on the same side as the athlete and not the coach. No feedback is necessary from the coach if the goals of the drill are explained at the beginning.

The blocker's hands are key. Blockers should always be able to see their own hands. This technique lends itself to one move straight over the net as opposed to a common error of swinging at the ball. Keep the head down and the eyes up. If the head comes back, the arms will follow. As stated earlier, vision of the attacker is very important. If the blocker watches the hitter, eventually the ball will come back into view. If the blocker is looking at the ball the head is back and the arms come off the

58

According to Giovanazzi, the block is the first line of defense; it takes away the opposition's preferred attack.

Photo: George Mason University

net.

Now move the box away from the net and toss the ball higher. Create a more gamelike situation where timing becomes more challenging. Continue to hit directly into their hands so that the challenge is timing and penetration of the plane of the net and not reading you.

To work on a two-person block, have a line of six players start in the middle front on the other side of the net. One is in the right front and a partner is in the middle front opposite the coach. The coach attacks into the two-person block.

FOOTWORK

For movement within 3 to 8 feet, a blocker should use a simple side step. By utilizing this type of shuffle, a blocker's hips never leave the net. For balls set further than 8 feet away, it is important to get there in a hurry. Basically, turn and run or use what is called a crossover step. Always lead with the foot in the direction you are going, then cross over and square up. The important aspects of this footwork are as follows: Make sure in the last step that you get the hip in the direction you are going back into the court. In other words, if you are going right, push your right hip into the court or else you will drift into another blocker or out of court. This footwork should be utilized for all skills. Always lead with your left foot if you are going left (foot to the ball).

Add this footwork to the progression. The more movement and challenges, the better.

A blocker should start the play a full arm's length off the net in case the ball is passed over. This distance from the net will allow space to attack the ball without netting.

Also what we call "Block Trips" really help with the utilization of this footwork. As part of your warm up each day, perhaps you can include a few trips along the net where players begin with side step, jump, side step. Progress into crossover steps with jumps. While using the crossover, make sure that your athletes keep their hands at their shoulder level; if they drop them too low, the likelihood of netting increases. Incorporate the block trips to ensure familiarity with the net.

BLOCKING SEQUENCE

A blocker should start the play a full arm's length off the net in case the ball is passed over. This distance from the net will allow space to attack the ball without netting. Once the blocker sees that the ball is passed well they should set up 2 feet off of the net. If a player is too close to the net, he/she cannot penetrate. Maintain this distance while you are moving. Vision and recognition of what is happening on the other side is the difference between knowing and guessing. As the ball is being played by the passer on the other side, read where that player's arms are facing. As the ball is being set, read the setter's hands and body and get a jump on where the ball will be set. Reading the setter is a lost art. Coaches can really give their blockers an advantage by teaching them to read certain body movements, which are signs to where the ball will be set. Finally, when the setter releases the ball and you know where it is going, take your eyes off the ball and pick up the approach of the attacker. The attacker will be drawing a line for you as to where they will attack the ball. See the pass, set and hit.

It is important, too, that we teach our blockers to recognize what they see. A bad pass probably means a high set outside which, in turn, more than likely means a crosscourt hit. Certain situations are indicative of certain outcomes. As blockers, our players should play those odds. Make educated guesses!

Finally, teach your blockers that recognition is the start of the entire play. A left-front blocker needs to recognize that a bad pass usually means a set to the opposing team's left side; therefore, he or she needs to transition from blocking to defense.

THE RESPONSIBILITY OF THE BLOCK

The block is your first line of defense. It needs to take away the opposition's preferred attack. We know that most people hit for the middle of the court and we know that the weakness of most blocks is the seam. A lot of work needs to be done to protect the area between the two blockers. Have them train together against live hitters, as well as the coach on the box. Next, we need the blockers to have a concept of what to give and what to take. Since the large majority of hitters attack seam and crosscourt, a good beginning philosophy is to teach blockers to take angle.

The end blocker needs to set the block. To take angle, we set the block up by putting the end blocker's outside hand on the ball. The middle blocker needs to get all the way out to the end blocker and close the seam. As the set is placed further off the net, the end blocker needs to move the block in. Force the attacker to hit the line, which on a deep set is a difficult shot. Keep in mind that attackers jump higher than blockers because they have an approach. Blockers need to jump after the hitter, especially as the ball is set off the net.

Middle blockers have a tough job. They need to be up on every legitimate attack. They are usually the biggest and should be the most mobile. I have seen a lot of very good middle blockers who are setters because they move so well. One characteristic that most blockers share is that they move to their right better than to their left. Make sure to balance the amount of work that your middle blockers do to both sides. You really cannot do enough block trips.

Keep in mind that the tight block with no holes is the goal. Second only to making sure the block is closed is the philosophy that you have to block the low, hard hit. Simply let the other team hit over you. Balls hit over tend to be softer and easier to dig. What has to be stopped is the low, hard attack that is too tough to dig. This is where the concept of playing the game on the other side of the net is vital. Stuffs occur as a result of blockers penetrating the plane of the net. It becomes one

The game of volleyball, like many others, has changed a great deal since its beginnings. Some of the greatest changes have been in blocking. Prior to the 1964 Olympic Games, reaching over the net to block was illegal and blocking was primarily defenseive and not strongly related to team success. But by the 1974 World Games, a team's blocking average correlated higher with tournament rank, win-loss ratio and percentage of games won than any other factor. In the 1984 Olympic Games, blocking was second only to spiking in determining team success.

(Farokhmanesh Ed.D., Mashallah and Carl McGown, Ph.D. A comparison of blocking footwork patterns. *Coaching Volleyball*, December/January 1988, 20.)

move, sealing the net, straight over.

During practice, I like to stand on the referee stand so that I can see if the hands are getting over. Nothing hurts the confidence of an attacker like a stuff block. Be patient as blockers; stuffs come in bunches. Keep in mind, too, that if a player has a tendency, he/she will go back to a favorite shot when times are tough and the score is tight.

TENDENCIES

The final component of great blocking is a scouting report that athletes can adhere to and execute. The coach's responsibility is to scout the opposition and know their preferred shots. Everyone has a tendency or a favorite shot. As a blocker, it is important to keep these assignments in mind, as well as the changes that take place in the course of a match. Keep in mind not only the individual tendencies but the team's preferred plays, as well. By being a mindful, intense blocker; if you are, points will come your way.

> The coach's responsibility is to scout the opposition and know their preferred shots. Everyone has a tendency or a favorite shot. As a blocker, it is important to kee these assignments in mind, as well as the changes that take place in the course of a match.

EXECUTION

The elements of blocking culminate in great execution. Mentality, vision, technique and knowing the opponent come together at the point of execution. As a blocker, once you have made a decision, go with it. Whatever you do in this skill, do with conviction. When in doubt, go all out! Penetration alone will win points for a team. If you can add the discipline that it takes to time the block well by waiting, seeing the hitter and taking away his or her best shot, success will come your way.

The goals accomplished by executing well are:

•Take away the opposing hitter's favorite or best shot.

•Block the low, hard shots so that your teammates can dig everything else.

•Force the opposing hitter to use a secondary shot. Make them beat you with a new shot. Remember, at the end of the game they will go back to their favorite shot.

•Get wide and move in -- as an end blocker, do not jump out and open up the seam.

•Challenge the opponent to hit line on deep sets.

•Know your scouting report!

•Be aggressive, dominant blockers.

•Remember what they ran last in this rotation and adjust.

•Control the net and be patient; blocks come in bunches.

•Look for your opponents to change their shot after a hitting error.

Greg Giovanazzi is the head women's volleyball coach at the University of Michigan (Ann Arbor, Mich.) and is a member of the USA Volleyball CAP cadre.

Section IV: Serve Receive

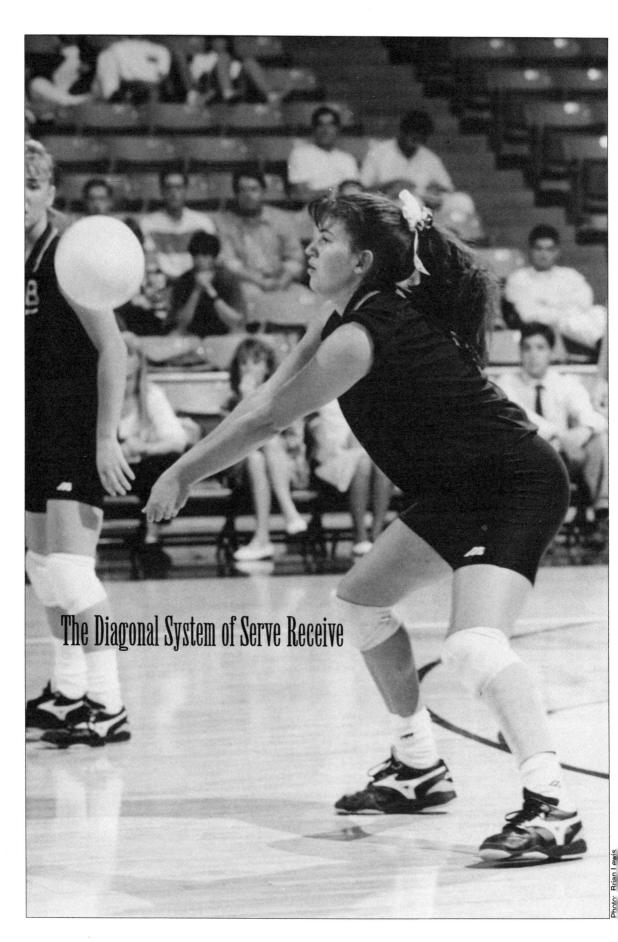

The Diagonal System of Serve Receive

Serve reception is the most important team strategy in volleyball. The ability to pass the opponent's serve accurately is critical to a team's success. Serve reception is most often used to convert the serve into an offensive strategy, even though the system may also be used to receive free balls. Traditional serve receive systems emphasize the use of a system of "zones" to be covered by individual players. This zone system commonly fails because a server may easily penetrate the seams of the zones with a strong serve, causing balls to land on the court untouched. It is also possible for players to collide with one another while going after the same ball because zone coverage responsibilities are sometimes unclear.

According to Davis, serve reception is the most important team strategy in volleyball.

TRADITIONAL ZONE SYSTEM

The most common formation for serve receive is the five-player or W-formation (see Figure 1) because it can be easily used with any offense. Using the zone approach, the LF, CB and RF all share the short serve coverage. The front-court zone responsibilities are equally divided among these three players. The back-court coverage is equally shared between LB and RB (Stokes and Haley, 1984). The zone system creates "seams" between players. Since these seams do not overlap, players rarely have the opportunity to back up each other. It is difficult for teammates to judge who should receive the serve, when the serve is in the seam area directly between them. Because of these seams, players frequently have a fear of colliding with a teammate. Also, the three front players (LF, CB and RF) tend to receive high serves which are either LB's or RB's responsibility.

DIAGONAL SYSTEM

The five-player W-formation is best played using the diagonal system of serve receive. In this system, diagonal lines of movement are utilized by all players (see Figure 2). The receivers move to receive the serve on diagonal lines (45 degrees) relative to the net. By using this system, the diagonals for each player are parallel to each other. Therefore, collisions between players are less likely to occur and decisions about which player is to receive the ball are more defined.

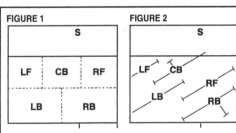

This system may also be used with two-, three- or four-player reception patterns (see Figure 3), but these patterns will have longer diagonals than the five-player system (Davis, 1990).

KEY CONCEPTS

1. The basic ready position is achieved with the arms extended forward, feet staggered along the diagonal, with the right foot forward, placing it closer to the target. The shoulders stay parallel to the net.

2. Individual receivers forearm pass from their left knee toward their

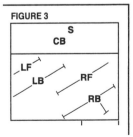

64

A wide base is much more stable when it comes to effective serve receive.

right knee as they move through the ball. This technique allows the direction of the pass to be in line with the target (in most offenses, the setter is right of CF).

3. All players move along their diagonals at least one step toward the path of the ball on every serve. By doing this, non-passing players also get a learning experience while creating an opportunity to back up the receiver.

4. All movements along the diagonal are performed with the same distance and depth between the feet. Slide steps or short, choppy steps are made along the diagonal to move toward the ball, while maintaining the distance between the feet. This wider base is more stable.

5. Everyone covers (passes) from high left to low right along their own diagonal. The front three receivers cover along their diagonal one deep diagonal left step and two short diagonal right steps. Deeper left steps would place these receivers in another player's area or attempting to play a ball which is going out-of-bounds. The two deep receivers cover to the inside shoulder of the other receiver. For example, if a serve is coming high and to the right of LF, it is CB's ball to receive; if a serve is low and to the right of LF, it is the LF's responsibility to receive it. Passing high right is poaching from another receiver who could pass the same ball in an easier position. (Exception: RB is the only player to cover high right to the deep corner for a serve toward the service box.)

6. RF is positioned so his/her diagonal passes between LB and RB, but only moves as far as RB's feet.

7. LF is positioned one meter from the left sideline and behind the attack line. LF covers short serves and protects the left sideline (high at waist level).

8. CB projects a diagonal line between LF and LB. CB's responsibility extends to the feet of LB. CB may also play one step toward the attack line for a very short serve to the middle.

9. Receivers on the right side of the court should be trained to take easy left serves slightly on their right to get a better angle toward the setter.

10. Diagonals can be "bent" to deal with different trajectories. For example, receiving a topspin serve which drops suddenly may require a slight adjustment forward from the normal diagonal (Davis, 1990).

In addition to the specific guidelines for the diagonal system, the following basic principles which are important for all types of serve receive patterns should also be applied:

1. the pattern must be appropriate for the level of play;

2. the team's strengths should be exposed (best passers) and the team's weaknesses should be hidden;

Volleyball coaches change their serve reception formations for many different reasons. Hiding a weak passer and running a quick attack are two of the reasons we have seen variations of the standard W formation. The most important consideration in deciding what pattern to use for serve reception is your team's ability to cover the court efficiently. The next most important consideration is that the setters be able to get to the desired area quickly eough. If either of these considerations is not met by the service reception being used, the coach's offensive system cannot be implemented at all. Thus, the serve reception being used must satisfy these two requirements.

(Shoji, Dave. (1987.) Service reception. *The AVCA Volleyball Handbook.* Indianapolis, IN: Masters Press, 161)

3. the pattern should be easy to practice;

4. the communication system between players should be consistent, using simple verbal ("mine," "my ball") and non-verbal cues ("open up" the body toward the receiver) [Neville, 1990]; and,

5. facing the net, the pattern should be shifted slightly to the left to defend against a majority of down-the-line serves.

PRACTICE

When practicing the diagonal system, it is best to start with two players and work on their serve coverage relationships first. Practice of the movement along the diagonals should begin without a ball to establish coverage responsibilities on the court. Then, a ball (served over the net) should be used to establish the spatial awareness of High Left to Low Right. A third, fourth and fifth player may be added to increase the "team" serve receive concept by moving along their diagonals to back-up teammates.

Even though this presentation has dealt with the traditional five-player W formation, this system can easily be adapted to a two-, three- or four-player serve receive pattern. It can also be adapted to an "M-formation," using three deep receivers and two front receivers to defend more against deep serving teams.

Different serve receive patterns may be used for all six rotations (see Figure 4). The number of players designated to receive the serve may be decreased to make communication less confusing and court responsibilities more defined (1991). However, using fewer players to receive the serve may also open up tremendous holes in the court coverage and the receivers will have to move greater distances to receive the serve.

SUMMARY

With the advent of the rally scoring system in volleyball (teams score a point for every rally won), serve receive and playing strong defense have become an integral part of a successful team. In rally scoring, a team no longer wins points only while they are serving. Now, receiving the serve successfully as a team becomes just as important as being a consistent serving team. The diagonal serve receive system will help to reduce errors caused by the miscommunication and undefined coverage, as is found in the traditional "zone" serve receive systems.

REFERENCES

Davis, K.L. *Volleyball*. Dubuque, IA: Kendall/Hunt Publishing Company, 1990.

Dunphy, M. and R. Wilde. *Volleyball Today*. St. Paul, MN: West Publishing Company, 1991.

Neville, W.J. *Coaching Volleyball Successfully*. Champaign, IL: Leisure Press, 1990.

Stokes, R. and M. Haley. *Volleyball Everyone*. Winston-Salem, NC: Hunter Textbooks, 1984.

Kathryn Davis, Ph.D., is an associate professor in the Physical Education Department at North Carolina State University in Raleigh, N.C.

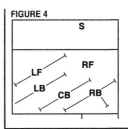

FIGURE 4

The receiving team always knows when the ball will be served. It cannot occur during a rally or as a surprise. The serve always takes place following a dead ball and after the official's whistle. Therefore, a routine can be developed to assist the receivers in being focused and ready. An example of a pre-reception routine is as follows: The official whistles for the serve and the receivers focus on the server; the server then tosses the ball and the receivers get down into their ready position. The receivers are then in the proper ready position, concentrating on the serve, ready to identify the type of serve and execute accordingly.

(Mueller, Ed.D., Lois. Effective serve receive techniques. *Coaching Volleyball*, December/January 1992, 12.)

The Philosophy of the Match-Up

The Philosophy of the Match-Up

TERRY LISKEVYCH

Terry Liskevych, head coach of the U.S. women's national team, recently took time out to share his thoughts on the concept of the match-up in volleyball, from the international game to high school. Following are his ideas on what young teams can do with the match-up, as well as the direction the U.S. team is currently taking.

CV: Taking into consideration the fact that some coaches may not be familiar with the concept, can you give the philosophy behind matching up, providing the significance of its success offensively?

TL: The first thing that I think is important is that you really do not look at what the other team is doing; rather, you look at what your strengths and weaknesses are and if you can establish a pecking order that fits within your philosophy of what is important in a volleyball match. There is no amount of time that you can spend describing the match-up—it depends on what level you are playing at and what wins at your level.

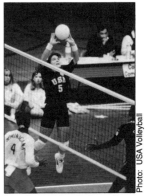

Photo: USA Volleyball

According to Liskevych, the match-up only works if you look at what your team's strengths and weaknesses are and then look at what the other team is doing.

As an example, in high school, serving is a very predominant indicator of who wins; therefore, maybe your match-up needs to have your three best servers lined up in a row to serve and that determines your rotational order. There are two different things that we are talking about— what is your rotational order of your players and what is the match-up against the rotational order on the other side of the court? But, first, I think you need to be really satisfied to ask, "What are the key ingredients to success at my level? If it is serving, then what do I do with it? If it is passing, what do I do with it? If it is blocking, what do I do with it?" For example, I look at the strengths of the U.S. team. The strengths are attacking the ball and blocking the ball. Those are then configurations by which we are going to line up based on the opponent. For example, if I am matching up against Cuba, I know that I want certain players being able to stop their top hitters, so I am looking at it in a blocking match-up.

Cuba is a very different team because it is almost a mirror image in rotations because they play a 6-2. So, their first three rotations are almost exactly like their fourth, fifth and sixth rotations, which does not happen unless you play a 6-2.

Very simply, international volleyball is a game where you have to find a way to side-out long enough to score points. Therefore, for us it is a combination of what are our blockers going to block and what are our best side-out opportunities against their blockers? Then it is a matter of knowing exactly how many points they have won and lost in each rotation and how many times they have a side-out in each rotation.

(Cuba is the only team internationally that plays a 6-2, so the players present less of a problem in match-up than other teams do.) Then, we look at who their key players are and figure out how we stop those people. We will match it up for our blocking scheme.

Very simply, international volleyball is a game where you have to find a way to side out long enough to score points. Therefore, for us it is a combination of what are our blockers going to block and what are our best sideout opportunities against their blockers? Then it is a matter of knowing exactly how many points they have won and lost in each rotation and how many times they have a side-out in each rotation. Those statistics are taken from a scoresheet. We total that against every team we play so that we know what we do in our rotations and what we do in their

Liskevych believes, at any, level, a team has to stop the opponent's top hitters.

rotations. In our statistics, we know that in our rotation one, we scored 11 points in 17 attempts so that is 65 percent. Our goal is to be above 40 in point scoring and if we are close to 70 in siding out, we are doing well. Of course, the permutations of the rotation are very complex. For each time they rotate, we can do a lot of other things and we are never going to truly match up 36 times. They are always going to be one off or one ahead, but we just try to see how often we can put our best siding out versus our points scoring in relation to what they are doing. It is a complex issue, but sometimes it works and it sometimes does not.

We can then go even more basic than that. For example, if we find a team that we are playing that is very susceptible to a down-the-line serve only in rotations two and five (because in those rotations their leftside hitter has to pull back to pass the ball), we serve the line and she is out of the play. I must figure out if I can do it so that my second and fifth rotation servers are my best line servers. Those are things that all become a factor.

The bottom line of everything we do rotationally is that we take all the times we have played and we look at our match up sheets (see Figure 1). (Before every match, one of our coaches puts all of our match-ups on a six-court grid—their blockers versus our side-outs so we have all of the possible situations. We have to have them in hand because during the game, if they start differently than we anticipated, then we have to pull another match-up out. We know stats for all of the times we have played and what the results were—won or lost in points and in games in every match-up. It is very complex.

CV: Do you have any basic principles of the match-up that you would like to address?

TL: The one I would address is how to stop the top hitters. That is still a big factor at any level because your opponent is going to put the ball down. Then, I would look at whom you use to attack their weaknesses based on both teams' serving and attacking. If the opponent has a short setter, maybe put your best or your "not-so best" hitter in who will have a field day. Regardless, your good hitter will have a field day anyway.

I never like matching up best with best because I do not want a neutral effect. I would like to maybe get my best against their weakest. But then you get your mediocre hitter who will not hit anything. Those are the types of things you must look at in the match-up.

I also think that in high school and college, a coach has fewer choices. I always say this in my clinics. I look a lot at a 5-1— identify whom you want to set

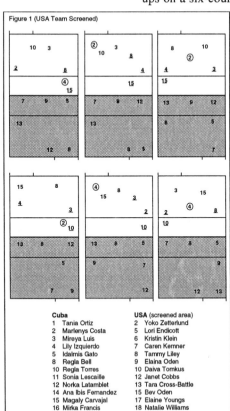

Figure 1 (USA Team Screened)

Cuba		USA (screened area)	
1	Tania Ortiz	2	Yoko Zetterlund
2	Marlenys Costa	5	Lori Endicott
3	Mireya Luis	6	Kristin Klein
4	Lily Izquierdo	7	Caren Kemner
5	Idalmis Gato	8	Tammy Liley
8	Regla Bell	9	Elaina Oden
10	Regla Torres	10	Daiva Tomkus
11	Sonia Lescaille	12	Janet Cobbs
12	Norka Latamblet	13	Tara Cross-Battle
14	Ana Ibis Fernandez	15	Bev Oden
15	Magaly Carvajal	17	Elaine Youngs
16	Mirka Francis	18	Natalie Williams

and everybody set her. You have to look at it as player-specific for you. I have always been a firm believer that you have to know your product because 99.9 percent of the time if your product plays well, it does not matter who is on the other side of the court.

CV: What is the most important aspect of the match-up for your coaching style?

TL: My statistical appreciation has always been very keen because I worked for [Jim] Coleman (USA Volleyball National Teams Training Center director), who developed all of the statistical systems in America. But, as a coach, I have always approached it the same way. Here are the statistics I am going to look at and then I follow my gut reaction. If the statistics imply what I am thinking, then I am going to say, "Okay, I am going to go with it." If it is totally opposite to what I am thinking, then I do not just accept that these are the statistics and we are going to go with this rotational order. It is a gut reaction. There are a lot of times that we will look at a match-up and we will say we have never tried it, but that will maybe surprise our opponent. So, we decide to go that way. There are only two or three teams internationally that really do this — USA, Brazil and occasionally the Russians. Most of the Asian teams never do. They never deviate one iota from the way they start. With Brazil, for instance, it is almost a comical game—we rotate and they rotate and it goes on. A lot of times you do not get the match-ups you really want.

I think that one of the fallacies in coaching is that you will only win if you get the match-up. There are a lot of other things that happen—if you pass, hit, serve, dig and block well, you are going to win. The tactical aspect of volleyball is much more important at our level than it is in college and moreso than it is in high school. In high school, you are going to have the elements of your skills taking over.

CV: Taking skill level into consideration, how do you teach players the principles of matching up? Do the setters call the plays or the hitters?

TL: Here the question is a little more complex because you have two different things in your offensive gameplan. My offensive gameplan is both sideout and transition. Those are two different things, so my setter gets to make the calls. In some cases, we are going to get very specific in certain rotations—we know what we can run against our opponent and she knows. I do not think you ever go to a setter and say, "You have to figure out every rotation." We are going to match you up so when you run these, you are going to be successful. I think we take for granted the different variables on the other side. The game is too quick. Most games that have a discriminatory variable like, for example football, evolve differently. You have a play and a time out and the coach is calling the play. The receiver has patterns, etc. In volleyball, boom, it happens!

In blocking, we have schemes by which our middle blocker knows what she needs to do to stop each rotation. Our end blockers now have choices themselves—am I blocking line or am I giving angle? They are also signaling to the team, "I am blocking line or angle," but if the ball is tight on the net, they must get the ball. Those are the strategies that are employed. In individual reads, there is more reading that goes on for the

The objective of an offense is to terminate the rally successfully. Coaches should use the most effective method to terminate the attack. Offensive strategies should be designed based on the premise of increasing the likelihood of success in offense.

The concept of offensive strategy is based on exploiting offensive strengths against an opponent's defensive weaknesses. The defense will attempt to neutralize an opponent by matching the team's defensive strengths with its opponent's offensive strengths. These concepts should be the basis of designing and implementing an offensive system.

(Welch, Mike. The three dimensions of offense: movements, locations and tempos. *Coaching Volleyball*, December/January 1995, 14.)

I always tell my players that if you have 12 players on a team and if six people are on, we are going to win the match. It is my job as a coach to find out who are the six that are on.

blockers because they see the opponent's offensive patterns and we know them.

How? We have a scouting report of all six of their rotations; we have spliced film for each rotation; and we have spliced film for each hitter. Then you discriminate; you say, "if I am in rotation two, what plays do they run?" That is the No. 1 thing you need to do simply because that will tell you what is going to happen. You have to look at these things in rank order—the pass (once the pass is passed you will know where they can set), then you have the setter and then every setter has tendencies — so you learn her tendencies. You know at a time-out juncture when they are behind to find out who they set or what play they run. As head coach, my job is to be in charge of the offense.

CV: Can you make an educated guess of how many hours it takes to go through all of the statistics to establish the correct match-up?

TL: In order to get a really good gameplan, I feel you need to get at least a week to 10 days of practice to be able to implement a good offensive gameplan and a really good defensive gameplan (see Figure 2). The irony of that is it never occurs. My philosophy has always been that in order for the American women to be good, we cannot concentrate on a technique game. It is a tactical game. The only time I have had arguments about this philosophy is with the staff that is no longer with me. They always thought they should be in the gym for 11 hours a day. We will never catch up to China, Japan or the Russians because they have been playing since they were 9 years old. Our kids have not played for that long, but tactically we can do some things. We have great athletes and we are competitive and intense. Therefore, we are a very tactically oriented unit.

CV: Obviously, the preparation for the match-up takes a very long time. After you have gone through the process, what if the match-up does not work?

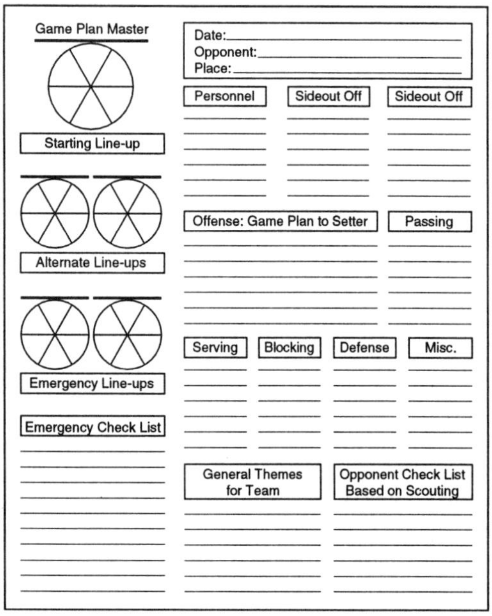

TL: You have to know why it did not work. If it did not work because you executed poorly, then you may go with that match-up again as opposed to the fact that in the match-up you executed well but they stuffed your lights out.

Is it an individual's lack in a match? I always tell my players that if you have 12 players on a team and if six people are on, we are going to win the match. It is my job as a coach to find out who are the six that are on. If only three are on, we may be in trouble because I might not have time in the match to find out which three are on and then determine which combinations to put them in. If an individual is having a terrible match, then we should still win.

Very simply, we look at it not so much as a match-up first. We look at it stats first. Are we passing badly because one passer is passing badly

FIGURE 2

Game Plan Master

Date:
Opponent:
Place:

Personnel | Sideout Off | Sideout Off

Starting Line-up

Alternate Line-ups

Offense: Game Plan to Setter | Passing

Emergency Line-ups

Serving | Blocking | Defense | Misc.

Emergency Check List

General Themes for Team | Opponent Check List Based on Scouting or are all of our passers are passing badly? Or in a certain rotation, is their server having a field day? Are we hitting badly? The one indicator of success at our level is hitting percentage. If our team hits above 35 percent, I think we have lost fewer than five matches, no matter what the other statistics say. The indicators we ask for right away include passing and hitting. What are we hitting? Where are we passing? Passing is so intricately connected to what we can run offensively. A team can have all of the nice offense it wants, but if no one is passing, a team cannot run some of these plays.

CV: How much of a variance is there in the personnel you choose to play against different teams?

TL: My philosophy has always been that you had better use everybody on your team or do not have them there, as opposed to only playing six. I know there are certain people who play very well against certain teams. Then it becomes a different situation of team strategy. For example, Asian teams are great ball control teams. Your job, then, as a coach, is to say, "Do I want to put a ball control team up against them or do I want to put up a team that is going to beat them at the net?" That is the way I would rather move. If you put a ball control team up against the Asians, they are going to "out ball control" you.

What is interesting is that the top four teams in the world will not win if two things do not happen—outside hitters have to be good and you had better be blocking the ball. Korea and Japan are the top two defensive teams in the world and neither is in the top four. So that means you have to win at the net right now. That does not mean that you do not play defense, but it is a lot easier when there is a good block up front. My discrimination is very simple. That is why I think the junior coaches and the high school coaches in America are spending a lot of useless energy spending time on individual defense as opposed to just a general ball control—ball control of the underhand variety and the setting variety. So we hit a lot of balls at people and teach them how to sprawl, roll and dive, but we do not teach them how to read a defense or a hitter. Nor do we teach them how to move on the court. If you really look at good teams, they move very little. If you are usually diving or sprawling or rolling, you are out of position or you are making it a great emergency move on a great play.

CV: What is the future of match-ups for the national team? Will it have a major impact?

TL: The future of match-ups is very exciting because of the whole computer integration with video and what that process can give coaches instantaneously in real time on a monitor where it can give you every hitter in every match-up possible. It is simply unbelievable. Statistics are the future of match-ups and I think we are way ahead of the world.

Terry Liskevych, Ph.D., is the head coach for the U.S. women's national team, which won a bronze medal at the 1992 Olympic Games in Barcelona, Spain.

Even after you have established an effective offensive lineup, you may find that in certain rotations your opponents are outscoring your team by a wide margin. Consequently, you must make adjustments. First, try switching blocking assignments or substituting for a weak blocker. Next, alter your own set selection. If these measures to not work, you may want to match up differently in the next game. You could rotate your lineup so as to match your best player against your opponent's best player. Another option is to match your best hitter against your opponent's weakest player or a short setter. Matching up is defintely worth a try.

(Nelson, Ruth and Frances Compton. (1987). Systems of play. *The AVCA Volleyball Handbook*. Indianapolis, IN: Masters Press, 140.)

Siding Out With a Two- or Three-Person Receive

Siding Out With a Two- or Three-Person Receive

BOB MAXWELL

The surest way to develop a winning program is to have a strong sideout offense. If you can sideout every time your opponents serve, they will not score a point, which greatly increases your chances of winning! I know this is unrealistic, but just imagine the ultimate fantasy: going through a season without giving up a single point.

Siding out is not only important, it is also misunderstood and underpracticed at many levels of play. We coaches work on fancy offenses with quick options and crossing patterns; we develop dozens of plays to confuse our opponents. In short, we spend hours of practice on the particulars of our great offense. Then in a match we let our opponents dictate the level of execution by letting them serve to weak serve-receivers.

Over the past dozen or so years, volleyball has changed drastically. Specialization has taken over. We have middle blockers, quick attackers, combination hitters, 5-1 setters, blocking subs, left-side players, right-side players, servers, defensive specialists, etc. It all depends on who you are talking to and what the system is. Most coaches and teams use some specialization.

Weak serve receivers can be detrimental to a great offense, simply because plays cannot be executed without a good pass.

SERVE RECEIVE SPECIALIZATION

Specialization is an outstanding idea because it can capitalize on each player's strengths while hiding weaknesses. But the most overlooked area regarding specialization is serve reception. Coaches look at players' abilities at the net (spiking and blocking) and decide where they should play. We design defenses to let our best defensive players dig the most balls and offenses to give our best hitters the most opportunities to attack with their best shots. But when it comes to serve reception (our primary means of preventing our opponents from scoring), we often just tell our players to pass to the target.

Specialization is an outstanding idea because it can capitalize on each player's strengths while hiding weaknesses.

Oh, we practice team serve receive for hours, but we defeat all of this practice because we still leave the targets (poor receivers) out on the court for our opponents to serve to.

Some of us may adjust our reception pattern slightly from rotation to rotation, but usually only with a play in mind or to give a quick hitter a better angle to attack from. These are valid adjustments, but if your team does not pass perfectly, then it is all for naught.

How do you scout an upcoming opponent? Do you chart sideout tendencies, free ball patterns and transition tendencies, identifying strong attackers along with serve receive strengths and weaknesses? Or do you just watch them play and decide to whom to serve? I would guess that the latter is most often true (and at the lower levels that is probably best). But think about it—if that is how you scout your opponents, they are probably scouting you the same way. Regardless of how they do it, they are always looking for serve receive weaknesses.

With this in mind, what can you do to give your team the best chance to win? Do you simply pray that your opponents guess wrong and go after one of your stronger receivers?

74

Serve receive specialization should be used for all levels for several reasons. First, serve receive is as important a skill as exists in volleyball. A team that cannot pass serve will not side-out and a team that canno side-out will lose. Given its importance, every possible step should be taken to ensure the most effective serve reception. Second, as with any skill, certain players perform better than others. Some teams are blessed with several good passers, while others struggle to find one, but there are distinctions in every group.

Third, five players are not needed to cover the court on serve receive -- in a game of doubles, two players can cover the entire court most of the time. Three players in a 9x9 meter area is plenty. Four is very safe. Five is often a crowd.

Which leads us to the fourth reason: Fewer receivers simplifies communication and reduces confusion. Most aces against a five-person receive are not caused by an inability to reach the ball but by hesitation among the passers. Fewer players means less traffic. Besides, non passers can learn to be excellent air traffic controllers, calling lines and the name of the most appropriate passer as the serve comes over.

Fifth, passing, like any skill, improves with successful repetitions. The more served balls that a player passes effectively from a position on the court, the more skilled he/ she will become in passing future balls from that position. For a player to reach and maintain her athletic potential, specific repetitions are crucial.

(Madden, Sean. Serve receive specialization. *Coaching Volleyball*, June/ July 1990, 14.)

I do not want to give my opponent charge of something I can control—which players will pass the most serves. I would rather adjust my reception patterns so that my weakest serve receivers do not receive serve at all and my strongest ones get all of the balls.

How can you accomplish this? First, identify your strongest serve receivers. You probably already know them, but to be sure, grade players for the first week or two of practice (have a manager or assistant coach score every ball that each player receives) and figure out the averages. The players with the highest percentages are probably your best serve receivers.

Second, familiarize yourself with the overlap rules, move your weak receivers out of the reception pattern (either to the net or the end line), and place your stronger receivers in high serve areas.

TWO- OR THREE-PERSON RECEIVE

I suggest that you use either a two- or three-person receive pattern, for two reasons. One, you reduce the number of players who must coordinate to pass serves effectively. Communication becomes easier. Two, you are now using only your best receivers and not giving your opponents a weak target to serve to. I have found that a few good, aggressive passers can cover the court better by themselves than if you give them "help" in the form of more players. By adding another player or two you decrease the good receivers' effectiveness by taking away their freedom to go get the serve!

For many coaches this philosophy is a radical change. But if you give your players the chance to do what they are capable of, you should see a marked improvement in your team's overall serve receive abilities. Remember, a strong and confident serve receiver who has more court to cover will pass better than a weak receiver with little court. Why let your opponent target your weak receivers? Take them out of the pattern and give the responsibilities of serve reception to your more confident and skilled passers.

Do not limit your players because you want to run "your" system—let your players' talents dictate the system. Do not decide they cannot do something; let them show you on the court what they are capable of. Often your players will be able to do much more than you thought possible, if you just let them go.

Probably the toughest thing to address when beginning to use a two- or three- person reception pattern is handling the non receivers. The serve receivers will bask in their extra responsibilities. However, the players relieved of serve reception responsibilities often rebel against the change. They feel you are making them less than a complete player, casting them out because they cannot pass.

I suggest you do two things to prevent such feelings from developing. First, explain to the non receivers that they still have passing responsibilities— after all, they still must pass free and down balls, and they are still integral to the team's defense. You are merely having the strongest passers receive serves, just as you have the best overhand passer set and other players attack according to their abilities.

Second, spell out the non receivers' new serve-receive responsibilities. In the front court, they will be your sideout quick attack or play-set hitters. Point out that now they will be able to concentrate on running different attack patterns and exploiting weaknesses in the opponent's block— and by doing so their kill percentages should rise dramatically. In the back court, they will call all of the serves in or out. Emphasize the importance of their jobs within the structure of the team's ultimate goal—to sideout!

According to Maxwell, players and coaches will have to adapt to a new system, requiring a different mindset.

ADAPTING

Not only will your players have to adapt to a new system, you will, too. Using two or three serve receivers requires you to have a different mindset. Serve receive practice will change. It will no longer be boring to practice serve receive; you can serve (or underhand toss) balls at your receivers and simultaneously run various interesting attack drills. You can work with setters while having receivers pass balls to them, rather than tossing perfect balls for them to set (setters trained with perfect tosses often cannot set when faced with imperfect ones in a match). This will give them practice setting "real" passes—it should improve your team's setting and reception, not to mention your attack.

Also, you will have to really think out your substitution patterns— otherwise you may feel you are trapped into a single lineup and cannot use your bench strength. Substituting is not difficult if you know your bench players' capabilities. You need to know how to adjust with each substitution.

For example, our left-side players are our primary serve receivers, but if a certain middle attacker is playing, she will replace one of the primary receivers in the back court because she is a very good receiver. This frees up another attacker to manipulate any weaknesses in our opponent's block while maintaining our reception abilities. This may sound difficult, but we were able to make the change in one walk-through simply by telling the team the adjustments. They accepted it and now know that when a certain lineup is on the court there is a slightly different reception pattern. This is nice, also, because by making one substitution, I change the look of our reception patterns, which can confuse the opponent.

Should you use a two- or three-person reception pattern? That is up to you and how you think your team will adapt to it. But whatever system you use to receive serve, remember that to increase your team's success at siding out (read winning), you dictate which of your players will receive the serve. Do not let your opponent control something that you can control.

Bob Maxwell is the head women's volleyball coach at the State University of New York, Buffalo (Buffalo, N.Y.) and is a USA Volleyball CAP Level II accredited coach.

Utilizing Your Best Receivers in Each Rotation

Setters set, hitters hit and passers pass. Arguably, passing is the most important of these; therefore, coaches often devise new serve reception and defensive strategies for our team each year.

Only in certain seasons are coaches blessed with three or four players who could pass serves and dig attacks at a respectable success rate. Most years, we have only a couple of these athletes. It makes sense, then, to place these players in reception and on defense where their abilities can best be tapped. Many high school coaches run reception and defensive formations without using their personnel to the fullest.

When two of the three passers are also the setters in a 6-2 offensive system, coaches may sprout a few prematurely gray hairs. Remember, we feel passing is most important. A secondary setter is used when your setters receive serve. You can train a player to make a basic set to one of your better attackers, thus keeping free your best passers.

Naturally, we have players whom we do not want to handle the ball much. As a result, we either hide them or place them in positions where few balls go. A coach must therefore be extremely creative. Very seldom does a high school team have a full cast of players with all of the skills.

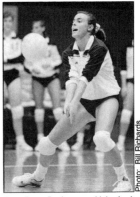

According to Braden, many high school coaches run reception and defensive formations without using their personnel to the fullest.

STARTING HOME POSITIONS
Player A

A is a 5'7" senior setter and second-team all-state player. She is an excellent setter and one of the top three passers. She plays strongside hitter and is one of three main attackers. When in the front row, A rotates to LB to receive the opponents' strongside attack. She blocks only on occasion. (Note: In our league, the opponent's weakside attack is insignificant. We do not waste a player on a double block. We single-block weakside until we consistently get burned.)

When two of the three passers are also setters in a 6-2 offensive system, coaches may sprout a few prematurely gray hairs.

Player B

B is a left-handed junior. She is a below-average passer, an average hitter and a good server. She only plays back row during her serve. Her substitute is an average passer and only plays back row. The sub is also a secondary setter for one service rotation. Neither receives serve unless it is necessary.

Player C

C is a 5'7" senior first-team all-state player. She plays middle hitter/blocker and is one of our top three attackers and defensive players. She jumps well and is very strong and aggressive. C plays the CB position on defense as our centerfielder and is one of our top three serve receivers.

Player D

D is a 5'3" freshman third-team all-state player. She fills our other

Braden believes coaches should place players in reception and on defense where their abilities can best be tapped.

setting position, is one of our three serve receivers and plays strongside hitter. She follows the same rules as Player A.

Player E

E is a 5'7" senior honorable-mention all-state player. She is left-handed, our third strong hitter and is an average passer. She makes our weak side strong. She plays a couple of defensive positions in the back row. E is a secondary setter in serve reception and receives serve on one rotation.

Player F

F is a 5'3" freshman back-row player and server. She is a very consistent server and an average back-row player. She never receives serve. Her front-row sub is a 5'9" sophomore who plays middle for us; she is an average hitter and blocker.

We use three primary players to cover most contacts. The other players play in positions that use their strengths and afford them success.

In these defensive alignments, we also single-block in the middle and on our opponent's weak side. We double-block the strongside attack. We always shift our serve reception to the left until we are beaten in the deep-right corner.

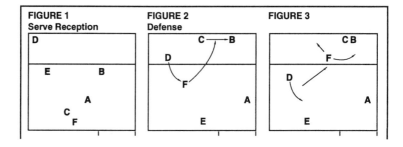

FIRST ROTATION

Serve reception: We use a four-person serve receive (see Figure 1). E and B take short serves. (The front two players on all of our four-person reception formations have short serve.) C and A receive most of our receptions. F hides. D (a main setter in our 6-2 offensive set) has first set, then moves to the strongside hitting position. A then moves to the RB position as our main setter. C and B are our hitters on the first attack. C hits middle. B (who is left-handed) hits weakside. After the attack, our players switch to their defensive home positions (see Figure 2).

Defense: C single-blocks our opponent's weak side and middle attacks. B and C block the strongside attack (see Figure 2). D's home position is two steps in front of the attack line. This gives D an opportunity to contest passes at the net, to block if needed and to move to a defensive position to dig the strongside attack. When C blocks the weakside attack, D covers for tip. F has the line or shifts right if the opponent's hitter hits cross-court on her attacks. We play normal player back defense when there is a middle attack.

When our opponents hit strongside, D reads the set and rotates to left-back position (see Figure 3). He/she reads and plays the attack. F charges to where he/she thinks the opponents will tip. A reads tip or line attack. E plays the attack according to a read on the attackers' approach, where the ball is set and where the block is set.

After the ball is played, D rotates to the strongside attack position, C to the middle attack position and B (a lefty) to the weakside attack (see Figure 4). A moves in for the set. If A plays the ball on first pass, B becomes our secondary setter. A, D and C are our three best receivers and defensive players.

SECOND ROTATION

Serve reception: B, the secondary setter, takes the first set; D and A serve receive (see Figure 5). E hits outside, D hits middle and C hits just to the right of middle. Again, we receive with four players.

Defense: Our defense for rotations 2 through 6 uses the same coverage as in the first rotation.

THIRD ROTATION

Serve reception: We again have a four-person reception. D takes the first set only (see Figure 6). A and C receive the majority of serves. B hides. If A or C has problems receiving, E moves back to receive and A or C hides.

FOURTH ROTATION

Serve reception: C and D receive most serves (see Figure 7). E takes first set as a secondary setter. A hits strongside. F hits middle off the reception. After E sets, he/she returns to the weakside position. D takes

Receiving the serve is undoubtedly the most critical skill for establishing a team's success. Perfection in passing depends upon both the team's skill level and the effectiveness and power of the opponent's serve. These factors, listed in ascending order of difficulty, should be considered when receiving the serve:

1. Avoid being aced; try at least to touch the served ball.
2. Make the pass playable. Get it in the air somewhere.
3. Pass the ball between yourself and the setter.
4. Target the pass to the setter.

If a team cannot side-out because of poor passing, change the receiving pattern. This alteration includes moving the pattern forward or back, flooding to one side or covering an ineffective passer. Any time passing is unsuccessful in a 6-2 offense, change immediately to a 4-2. The best passers should be in optimum position to receive the statistically highest percentage of serves (near the middle of the court). In tense situations, strong passers should extend their range and cover extra court area in addition to assuming the responsibility for getting the ball passed. In extreme situations, the best passers can take every serve.

(Nolen, Marilyn. (1987) Tactics and strategy in volleyball. *The AVCA Volleyball Handbook*. Indianapolis, IN: Masters Press, 111.)

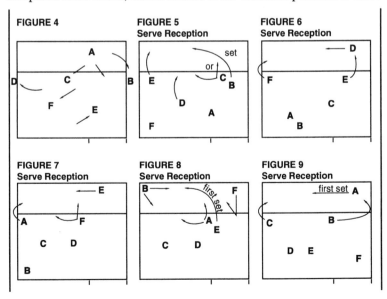

FIGURE 4

FIGURE 5
Serve Reception

FIGURE 6
Serve Reception

FIGURE 7
Serve Reception

FIGURE 8
Serve Reception

FIGURE 9
Serve Reception

on her setting role. B hides. If C or D has problems receiving, we rotate A into the reception and hide C or D.

FIFTH ROTATION

Serve reception: Again we use a four-person reception. B hides at the net (see Figure 8). Once the ball is served, B moves along the net to her weakside hitting position. C and D receive most serves. E is the secondary setter and sets first ball. A hits strongside and F hits middle on first attack. After our attack, our players go to their home defensive positions. Again, if C or D has reception problems, we rotate A into the reception.

SIXTH ROTATION

Serve reception: A takes first set (see Figure 9); D and E receive most serves. If E has trouble receiving serve, we shift to the formation shown in Figure 10. C and D then receive serve and we give up the short serve to the left front.

Using individual player strengths to full advantage opens channels to individual success; in turn, the team success is heightened.

No substitution for E is completed simply because if E's substitute is not as good as E, why sub for him/her? Instead, have one of your better passers step over and pass. Put the pressure on the serving team to short-serve to the open spot. Force them to serve to your better passers. If they beat you at this, they deserve the point.

SUMMARY

A, C and D do most of the receiving and A, C, D and F are in the primary defensive attack areas. You would have to rethink them for a faster attacking system. With this system, we feel we use our athletes' strengths to full advantage. This opens channels to individual success, which, in turn, affects the flow of team success.

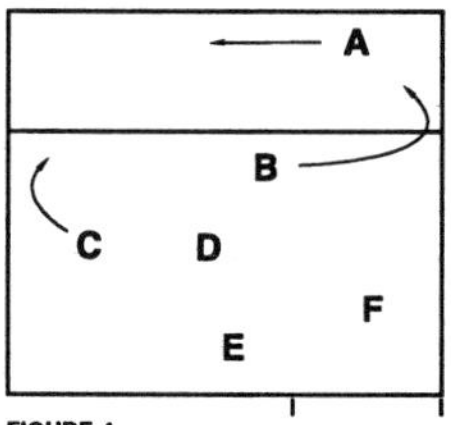

Chuck Braden is a volleyball coach with the New Knoxville Volleyball Club in New Knoxville, Ohio.

FIGURE 10

A

B

C   D

F

E

FIGURE 4

Section V: Defense

Developing and Communicating About Defenses

Developing and Communicating About Defenses

SEAN MADDEN

At the end of our second day of 1988 preseason practices, we were wrapping up with a wash drill pitting our anticipated starting lineup against the reserves with my new assistant coach, a standout defender and setter in a Top-20 program, running the second team offense. This would be the day she would begin showing my young team, just entering its second year of NCAA Division I competition, what playing tough is all about. As the teams huddled on the court, the left back on each side called a defensive alignment utilizing an early ver-sion of our Gonzaga numerical system for

Madden believes the only really important element of defense is digging the ball.

labeling defenses. My assistant said nothing; she was focused on making the initial competitive impression we had talked about earlier in our morn-ing staff meeting. She was fired up to play. Three or four rallies into the action our big gun leftside hammered a lineshot by the block in front of the assistant who, located halfway deep down the line, cut right in front of our middle back who had rotated to the line. She passed a dime to the right front who lofted a money set which the left side buried. My assis-tant was obviously pleased. So were most of her teammates. The one exception was the junior defensive specialist who had rotated to the line as called for in the system being played, only to be cut off by her new assistant coach. Confident of her understanding of our systematics, the DS strode directly to the assistant and said, "Nice dig, but you were in the wrong place. We are in 2357 and you are supposed to get tips." With a look of utter disbelief (and perhaps a touch of disgust) the assistant blurted, "I do not care what defense we are in. I play dig-the-ball defense!" She then summarily spun and strutted to her starting position.

I begin with this story because my assistant made a very important point that day which I must pass on as a preface to this discussion of defensive systematics. The point: The only really important element of defense is digging the ball. "Dig-the-ball defense" is the ultimate and sole goal for every team when the opponent is about to attack. Systems cannot dig balls; players dig balls. Systems are valuable only to the ex-tent that they facilitate players and make them a coordinated group of great individual defenders. Thus, there are two distinct components of dig-the-ball defense: 1) getting defenders in position to touch balls; and 2) training defenders to dig balls to target. This discussion of the Gonzaga system for developing and communicating about defenses is presented as a means of improving efforts in the former area. Please heed the caveat that the latter area is far more important, though not discussed here.

Warnings aside, what I will discuss here is a precise system for com-municating about defenses which we have developed over the past sev-eral years at Gonzaga University. It is offered here as a possible standard, but more likely as a model for other programs to create their own mecha-

84

A great pair of hands on a tall player makes for a very good setter.

Offense captures an audience's immediate attention; defense wins matches and eventually wins championships. The best defense combines two factors: sound techniques (in blocking and individual defense) and teamwork (to take as much of the floor as possible away from the opposition). The best team defense reacts quickly and spontaneously to the requirements of any situation.

(Liskevych, Terry and Bill Neville. (1987) Floor defense: back court defense. *The AVCA Volleyball Handbook*. Indianapolis, IN: Masters Press, 195.)

nisms for more meaningful communication about what they and their opponents are doing in the area of defensive systematics.

THE NEED FOR EFFECTIVE COMMUNICATION ABOUT DEFENSES

Traditionally in volleyball we have heard the terms "perimeter" or "white," "middle up" or "red" and "rotational" or "blue" to describe various defenses. We also describe blocks as taking "line" or "angle" or "splitting the ball." The question is: Do these terms completely describe the varied defenses we now see in our game and, more importantly, are they adequately descriptive to direct our teams effectively during a high-pressure match?

The rapid development of offensive options such as swing hitters, one-leg takeoffs and back-row attack has elicited a bevy of new defensive approaches employed by various coaches. While there once were three basic defensive formations with small variants, there are now multiple and major variations. As each team creates its own defensive system, it is helpful to be able to describe any idiosyncrasies or options succinctly. Furthermore, the days when a team could use the same basic defense against every opponent are long past at higher levels of play where varying offensive approaches virtually force opponents to adapt. Reliance on players instinctively freelancing within a broad general system also seems risky given the against-the-flow shots generated by swing and one-leg attackers. As the need to play multiple defenses increases, so does the need for a viable, efficient method of communicating about those defensive choices.

THE FOUNDATIONS OF THE SYSTEM

The Gonzaga defensive codification system is based on alphanumeric labeling of zones on the court. As such, it is similar to offensive systems already in use in our sport. The Coleman System of labeling nine net zones using digits 1 through 9 is perhaps the best-known example. The Selinger System of nine zones using digits 0 through 5 and letters A through C is similar. Finally, the backcourt attack zone breakdown made popular by the USA men's national team utilizing letters A through D and "pipe" applies alphanumeric coding.

Through the years, many coaches have in fact used a numeric system for referring to defensive zones. They have simply applied the same six-zone (1 through 6) system as used to refer to service order and serving target areas. The only problem with this system is that the zones are too large to allow meaningful distinctions in many cases.

The value of alphanumeric labeling is that the codes are simple, progressively ordered and easily memorized. Use of code is superior to use of descriptive language due to its terseness and superior precision once initial definitions are agreed upon.

Though diagramming can be superior to vocal codes, especially for visual learners, the lack of time and proximity of coach to players inherent to the game of volleyball clearly limits the utility of such diagrams during actual match play. Whenever diagrams can be used in conjunction with codes there is a decided advantage. This is particularly true during the initial teaching of the codes; you should discover this yourself as you look at the figures included with this article in order to understand fully the codification system being presented herein. Before that system is delineated, it is important to describe the phases of defense to which it applies.

Through the years, many coaches have, in fact, used a numeric system for referring to defensive zones. They have simply applied the same six-zone (1 through 6) system as used to refer to service order and serving target areas. The only problem with this system is that the zones are too large to allow meaningful distinctions in many cases.

THE PHASES OF DEFENSE

Defensive positioning in volleyball typically occurs in three phases. Different coaches use varying titles to refer to these phases, but they are generally in agreement over the order of occurrence. First, players assume "starting positions" during the opponents' first contact of the ball. These starting positions serve two purposes: 1) as functional digging positions for attacks which do not allow time for adjustment to other positions, e.g. setter dumps and quick hits; 2) as convenient central positions which allow efficient movement to actual digging positions for higher sets. Following the set, players move to "read positions" based on the team system being used to defend against the given set. Generally, teams will have separate read positions dictated for left-side, right-side and second-tempo middle sets, as well as systems to defend against downballs and freeballs.

Once a player has moved from starting position to read position, he/she generally will make small adjustments based on the hitter's actions and the blockers' positioning before assuming an "adjust position" just before the attacker contacts the ball.

THE GONZAGA DEFENSIVE ZONE GRID

For purposes of referring to the areas to which defenders are deployed and areas "shadowed" by the block, the Gonzaga system divides the court into 9 zones with each having a distinct alphanumeric label (Figure 1). These zone reference codes remain the same for all phases of defense and all types of sets being defended against. The dividing lines between zones are clearly marked for diagramming purposes only. In reality, these must be seen as flexing delineations. Players must recognize the purpose intended in digging or blocking certain areas and strive to achieve that pur-

NET

1	8	7
2	0	6
3	4	5

FIGURE 1 - The Gonzaga Defensive Zone Grid

86

pose without getting caught up on linear distinctions between zones.

STARTING POSITION CODIFICATION

Each of the six players on the court assumes a starting position within the team's system whenever the ball passes over the net to the opponent's side. Using the Gonzaga system the starting positions of the three backcourt players are listed from left to right as three alphanumeric labels. Thus, 246 would be a typical triangle formation where the players have the option of being shallow in those zones or staying deeper in perimeter. This and additional formations are depicted in Figure 2 along with their codification.

Because the positioning of blockers is not determined by defensive areas covered but by the opponent's potential points of attack, in the Gonzaga system, blocker starting positions are designated using the nine numbered net zones of the Coleman System (you could just as easily apply the Selinger system if that is what you use for offense). Because the Coleman zones ascend in order from left to right for the offense, for defensive reference they should descend from left to right (see Figure 3). Thus, we refer to a blocker "fronting" the opponent's attack zone and use the number of that zone to indicate his/her location. As is the case with the backcourt defenders, the alignment of the three blockers in starting positions is listed beginning with the left blocker and ending with the right. If the positions are listed as 663, then the blockers are positioned so that the left and middle are side-by-side, fronting a likely "one" attack, while the right blocker is pinched in to help against a "31." This and other possible blocker starting positions are displayed in Figure 4 along with their codification using the Gonzaga system.

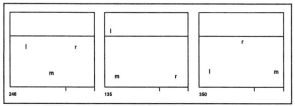

FIGURE 2 - Typical backcourt starting positions with codes.

READ POSITION CODIFICATION

To specify where defenders deploy against specific sets the nine floor zone system is again applied. Because defenses are built around the block, the first application is to define how the block will be aligned. A single zone number is used to refer to the deep zone which will be in the seam of the two blockers in a double-block situation. If the block closes and does its job the two adjacent zones should also be protected by the block. For example, against a left-side attack a right-side blocker setting up a standard block that allows true line and power angle will call or signal "4" then place the block so that she protects zone 5, the middle protects zone 3, and they combine to protect zone 4 with their seam. The same blocker planning to take the line will call or signal "5" thus protecting zones 4 through 6. On the other hand, she would call or signal "3"

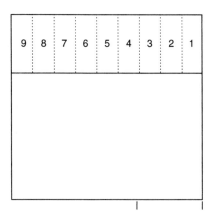

FIGURE 3 - Blocker starting position zones (Coleman's offensive zones mirrored).

to create an inside block that protects zones 2 through 4 taking away power angle and allowing inside line. If the plan is to get just one blocker up on a particular attack, the zone called is still the one that would be in the seam, but the defenders now know to cover that zone as it will remain open.

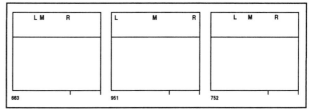

FIGURE 4 - Typical blocker starting positions with codes.

Once the block is designated, the deployment of the remaining four players in digging positions is described by listing two two-digit numbers beginning with the off- blocker's zone followed by the left back's, the middle back's, and ending with the right back's position. Using this system, a standard perimeter defense against a left-side attack would be a "12-46" while a rotational would be called "23-57." These and other defenses that are often seen are depicted with their codes in Figure 5.

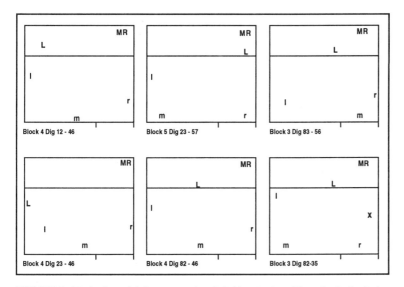

FIGURE 5 - Typical read defenses against leftside attacks with codes indicated.

ADJUST POSITIONING

Once educated in the system, players will understand that the alignment of the block will dictate the purpose and adjust positioning of backcourt defenders. For example, if the block is a "4" and the defense is "12-46" against a left-side attack, then the middle-back defender will know that his/her purpose is to align in the seam and defend over the top of the block while the left back will realize that he/she should read off the inside of the middle blocker to dig the power angle. Meanwhile, the right back reads off the outside of the block to defend the true line and off-speed over the top and the off-blocker watches for tight angle attacks and inside off-speed.

There are three components to the philosophy of defense: the right attitude, an appreciation of tactical considerations (the role of the block and the placement of diggers) and effective communication.

You must instill in your players the attitude that no ball wil hit the floor at any time, that no ball is impossible to retrieve and that every ball will be played with maximum effort every time. No value judgment on whether or ot a ball is playable is ever made during a play. The athletes simply play as hard as they can and make every effort on each sequence until it is terminated. We call this behavioral attitude relentless pursuite. Relentless pursuit means that each player believes "every ball comes to me" and "I will play every ball." This conditioning will heighten players' levels of concentration and physically prepare them to respond. Before you will be able to condition your players to believe they will play every ball, you will first have to convince each player that, "While I am in my defensive area, I will position myself so that every ball will come to me."

(Liskevych and Neville, 195.)

USING THE SYSTEM TO CREATE YOUR TEAM'S DEFENSE

The first and most obvious use for the Gonzaga defensive codification system is to deploy your own team defense. Rather than train defenders to always play just one starting position and one read position, the system allows the creation of numerous options which can be employed to stop the opponent's most notable tendencies.

Priorities which should be considered in the formulation of a defensive system are: stopping the best shots of a particular hitter or group of hitters on the opponent team; choosing the most effective role for your block (stuff opponent's best shot or channel to your best defenders); placing your best defenders where the most balls will go; placing each defender where he/she is at their best (close to point of attack v. far; digging off-speed v. digging hard shots); limiting travel distance between starting position and read positions for each player within the system; minimizing setter penetration distance from digging position to target position; and facilitating effective transition offense from the assigned defensive positions.

For example, prior to a fall 1990 match, our analysis of videotapes indicated that the opponent's setter often executed a right rotational dump to 1 while the middle attackers typically hit to 3 and 5. Consequently, we adjusted starting positions to those locations (135). Analysis of set distribution tendencies showed that 60 percent went to the left side while 30 percent went to the middle and only 10 percent to the right-side hitter. Consequently, we decided to start our left blocker fronting 6 and have her commit on the middle while the middle blocker would front 5 where she could both assist against the quick attack and get outside easily. The right blocker would front 3 to assist against 31s but released immediately to front 1 when the middle attacker initiated an inside approach. Analysis of the outside attackers showed that the left-sides liked to hit toward 3 (deep corner angle) and 2 (power angle) with some inside offspeed to 8, but their balls were seldom hit well enough to be undiggable. Therefore, we chose to block 5 and defend 82-35 which would take away all of the lefts' favorite shots while being a simple defense to move to given our commit blocking and starting position alignment. Against the right side attacker we anticipated having just one blocker or a late double block taking 5 and planned to dig 62-35. This entire gameplan is delineated in Figure 6. While we had minimized movement for all of our defenders,

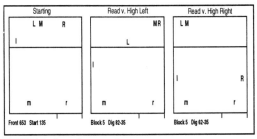

FIGURE 6 - Sample gameplan.

the one major drawback to our choices was the need for our setter to penetrate from 5 to target; for a standout quick, 6-foot setter this was surmountable while it might not have been for others.

The ease of making these changes came from having taught our players the terminology that allowed specific communication and the fact that we had practiced playing all of these positions from day one of practice. This was much different than pre-system days when we would say "shade" here or "shift" there and hope to be able to adjust from more ingrained "standard" positions. Of course, as our opponent adapted to our defenses during the match, we were able to change defensive alignment just as quickly. For example, when their left sides began to tip over the top of the block to 7, we quickly changed to a 3 block and an 83-56 defense with the line digger staying shallow enough to pick up balls in 7. Based on shot charts kept during the match, we also made a change in the starting position of our middle back from 3 to 4 against one middle attacker while leaving her in 3 against the other.

It might be wise to start in a defense which you plan to abandon quickly, as most opponents chart your defense early then assume it will remain constant. You can then change to the defense called for in your pre-match scouting report.

There are actually several factors that should be considered as automatic triggers for changes in defensive deployment: The rotation of the setter from front to back row might influence starting positions; the rotation of outside attackers may dictate different read positions against left sets; the rotation of middle attackers may call for different starting positions; specific sets or set-tempos or attack combinations might elicit changes in starting and read positions; and known and anticipated opponent strategies or tendencies such as going offspeed at crunch time might call for planned defensive variations.

Something to consider in the selection of defensive deployment is the merit of change for the sake of catching opponents off-guard. It might be wise to start in a defense which you plan to abandon quickly, as most opponent's chart your defense early then assume it will remain constant. You can then change to the defense called for in your pre-match scouting report. A related strategy is to switch defenses arbitrarily at time or points-scored intervals just to keep the opponent's hitters off-balance. This can be particularly effective in the case of block alignment.

METHODS FOR CALLING THE DEFENSE

With the use of multiple numeric codes, calling of defenses could obviously get confusing unless clear systematics are established. We always precede blocker starting positions with the word "front" and back-row starting positions with the word "start." We always lead read blocking alignment codes with the word "block" to prevent confusion with backcourt deployment. We precede defensive read deployment codes with the word "dig" for the same reason. Finally, we attach "right" or "left" to distinguish whether we are talking about our alignment against the opponent's left- or right-side

There must be ongoing, clear communication during all defensive situations. Coupled with the communication must be the consistent adherence to the rules of defense.

Furthermore, the same trigger word must be used. There are three types of communication:
1. The communication of direction.
2. The communication of execution.
3. The communication of confirmation.

It is not always necessary to use the three types in every situation, but your players must be trained and prepared to use the communication necessary to complete a smooth play. Each type of communication uses different trigger words.

Communication of Direction

Trigger words include:
•Switch - the middle back on a high ball would change with either wing to present optimal digging.
•Rotate - a defensive captain call movement.
•Tip - alerts an adjustment.
•Deep - stay on perimeter.
•White or Back - which type of defense to use.

Communication of Execution

Trigger words include mine, me or ball - an execution trigger word such as mine should be uttered every time by the player about to make contact.

Communication of Confirmation

Trigger words include yours, okay, (Name) - all confirm that the ball belongs to the other player.

Communication should be monosyllabic, concise and clear. One of the most devastating blows to a team's tempo is losing a point or serving opportunity because of a failure to communicate.

(Liskevych and Neville, 198.)

attacks. If we are using specific alignments for individual sets, then we attach our audible name for that set. For example, before the match a coach will give the gameplan, saying, "Front 663 and start in 246. Block 4 left and dig 12-46. Block 3 right and dig 61-35."

During the course of the match, we designate our middle blocker as the person who is allowed to change blocking alignments and our left back as the defensive captain who changes digging positions. They make changes whenever they desire and communicate them to the team on the court. Of course, the two must check their calls with each other to avoid non coordinated blocking and digging.

USING THE SYSTEM TO CODIFY AN OPPONENT'S DEFENSE

The second advantage of the Gonzaga system is that it allows quick and easily understood codification of the opponent's defensive alignments. Rather than having to wait for a timeout to diagram where they are positioning or using vague terms, specific codes can be yelled to the players on the court immediately and, due to their training in the system, they will compute them quickly. This results in the players having insight into what shot options will likely work and which will not.

For example, if we tell the team that the opponent is blocking 5 and playing 23-57 against our left attack, our hitters will immediately know that they should attack angle and use some inside tips. On the other hand, if the opponent is blocking 3 and defending 13-56, we will resort to tips over the top and to the middle while anchoring the line digger with hard shots in his/her direction.

Telling our setter that the opponents start with their blockers fronting 661 will signal him/her to run slides and other quick options behind rather than 1s and that 31s will also work. Telling the middles that the backcourt players start in 246 and charge will cause them to attempt attacks to the deep corners, 3 and 5.

USING THE SYSTEM TO DESIGNATE SPECIFIC SHOTS

We have all had attackers become very frustrated when they cannot seem to find any shot that will work. Using the Gonzaga codes to give them a specific shot that should surely work is a means of helping them escape the frustration. For example, an outside hitter could be told to tip 8 against a 23-46 defense. Or, in the case of individual defenders attempting to cover multiple zones, we might tell the hitter to mix it up between 1, 2, 8 and 0 to keep the opponent's off-blocker off balance. If their shots are being dug deep, middles will jump at the chance to tip 1 once told it is open. And every setter can benefit from being told to dump 1 when the left back is serving.

The locational codes can also be used to tell hitters what shots will not work and where specific defenders are located, who should be picked on because they are weak or in order to take them out of the transition attack, e.g. the setter.

FURTHER REFINEMENT OF COMMUNICATION

As is the case with the creation of boundaries to define anything, there are vague and gray areas involved in this codification system. Often defenders need to be or are aligned between two zones. Other times they may be at different depths within a single zone. Consequently, we have adopted several terms that provide more precise locational detail:

• Perimeter—On or near a sideline or endline. Example: Stay perimeter in 2 against the left = be on the sideline in the power angle.

• Shallow—Toward the front end of a zone in relation to the attacker. Example: The right back is in shallow 6 against our left = she is down the line but not much deeper than the 3-meter line.

• Release—Go to in a given situation. Example: Release to 8 on an off set = a player digging in 1 will move to 8 on a set that is too far off the net for the opponent to hit tight angle.

With the freedom to adjust within the system, great individual defenders will rise to their potential.

• Shade—Stay to one side of a zone. Example: Dig 4 shading 5.

• Cover—Choose among two or more zones. Example: Cover 1 and 2 = choose anywhere in the tight or power angle depending on judgment of the situation.

LIMITATIONS AND FURTHER CAVEATS

After several years, we are still constantly refining and adjusting the Gonzaga system. In fact, we started with a nine-zone system, expanded to 13, then reverted back to nine, as you will note if you read the original version of this article in *Coaching Volleyball* (December/January 1993). We use and emphasize different components each year depending on our personnel and what works best at that time. After several years of experimentation and application, we are well aware of the system's pitfalls and limitations

First, it is paramount that each player understand as explained earlier that systems do not dig balls, they do. Multiple deployment options can get them in the warzone, but only great individual defense can stop the barrage of missiles from opponents.

It is also important that every player remember that the ball is far more important than any number; they must stop and dig where they are when the ball is being struck rather than be caught moving to where they are supposed to be within the team system. Furthermore, it is crucial that players feel free to make choices and adjust spontaneously to what is happening out on the court. If a coach is adamant that the player assigned to dig 3 must always be in 3, that player may miss multiple opportunities to dig balls in 4 or 0 that he/she might otherwise have gotten. Our rule is that the player must move to the assigned zone when the ball is set, but then he/she must use instinct to adjust prior to contact by the attacker within that zone or into adjacent zones that are not assigned to other players. The bottom line is that the player has to find a way to dig some balls.

With the freedom to adjust within the system, great individual defenders will rise to their potential. Team systems should always be chosen with an eye toward maximizing that potential by funneling balls to the great defenders and keeping them away from the weak ones.

Of course, the team's ability to be effective in playing multiple defenses and switching from one to another is directly dependent on training time involved in that process. Defensive and gamelike drills must be incorporated that call upon athletes to play in different systems, change the system during play and adjust individually within the system.

Sean Madden is the head women's volleyball coach at Gonzaga University in Spokane, Wash.

Motivation for Floor Defense

Former national team assistant coach Bill Neville asserted that attitude governs the success of a defensive player (Neville, 1990). UC Santa Barbara Head Women's Volleyball Coach Kathy Gregory contends that a player with intense motivation can play good defense, even if the player only posseses average skill (*AVCA Volleyball Handbook*, 1987).

Having the right attitude is just one of three components in Neville's formula for creating successful floor defense. The other two parts of the equation include an appreciation of tactical considerations with specific regard to the placement of the diggers and effective communication.

This article will define motivation in a model format, focusing on motivation as it relates to the quality of a team's floor defense. By investigating the various aspects of motivation, appropriate steps toward improving individual and/or team behavior modification can be implemented.

Having the right attitude is one component in the formula for creating successful floor defense.

THE MOTIVATION THEORY

Vroom's Expectancy Theory (VIE), a process theory of motivation, is the framework for defining the motivation of a player who executes floor defense skills. Vroom's models explain performance on the basis of outcome. The terms valence, instrumentality and expectancy are used to determine motivation.

Simplified, the theory states that motivation (M) is a product of valence (V), instrumentality (I) and expectancy (E): $M = V*I*E$

VALENCE

Valence is the attraction one has to acquiring a goal. The valence continuum ranges from an athlete wanting to dig every ball (high goal acquisition) to having no desire to dig any ball (low goal acquisition).When converted to a numeric value, the attraction can range from 1.0 to -1.0. If a player states that an event is attractive or desirable, it might be assumed to have a positive valence. A negative valence would be described as having unattractive or undesirable events (Vroom, 1964).

INSTRUMENTALITY

Instrumentality is the method of obtaining a goal. The instrumentality continuum ranges from an athlete with elite athletic ability and technical skill (high instrumentality) to having no athletic ability and technical skill (low instrumentality). When converted to a numeric value, the ability can range from 1.0 (high instrumentality) to 0.0 (low instrumentality). The cognitive perception of an individual's instrumentality also affects performance (Vroom, 1964).

Expectancy is the level at which a player envisions reaching a goal. The expectancy continuum ranges from an extremely confident player who expects to make every play (high expectancy) to a non-confident player who does not expect to dig a ball and has an "I cannot do it" attitude (low expectancy).

EXPECTANCY

Expectancy is the level at which a player envisions reaching a goal. The expectancy continuum ranges from an extremely confident player who expects to make every play (high expectancy) to a non-confident player who

96

Photo: North Dakota State

According to Welch, the instrumentality of a player is derived from combining physical testing results with a coach's own evaluation of the player's defensive skill level.

does not expect to dig a ball and has an "I cannot do it" attitude (low expectancy). When converted to a numeric value, player confidence can range from 1.0 (high expectancy) to 0.0 (low expectancy). If a player states that an outcome has a 50-50 chance of following the act, the assumption is an expectancy value of 0.50 (Vroom, 1964).

MATHEMATICAL PRODUCT

After the creative process of assigning numeric values to valence, instrumentality and expectancy, these figures can be multiplied together, its product representing the level at which a player is motivated for floor defense.

Upon analysis, it is easy to see that a negative or low value in any of the three categories will cause this motivational product to be low or negative. Thus, the theory inherently states that motivation can only be as strong as its weakest link. For example, an athlete could have the skills (high instrumentality) and expectations (high expectancy) to play great defense, but, for whatever reason, has no desire to dig a ball (low valence). In this case, the likelihood of the athlete digging the ball is low.

While quantifying the aspects of motivation is difficult, the results may be of value to the coach and player when determining which aspects of motivation need to be improved.

Further, Vroom states performance (P) is a product of ability (A) multiplied by motivation (M) (Vroom, 1964): $P = AM$. He postulates that the internal drive of a person to exert a given amount of effort in performance is a function of the algebraic sum of valences and expectancies (Vroom, 1964).

METHODS OF MEASUREMENT

The methods of measurement include subjective as well as objective methods. Objective methods include observations of players as they execute floor defense skills (personal or videotape). Videotape analysis can provide in-depth data as to what defensive plays are being executed and what type of attacks are not being successfully dug.

Coaches should exercise caution in treating the results of the questionnaire as absolute values. Bias may exist in the way questions are written and interpreted, as well as the propensity for people to answer these types of questions in a socially acceptable manner.

Subjective methods include personal interviews where players are asked to verbalize their levels of desire and expectancy in both general and specific situations. Open-ended questions are created to illicit player descriptions of their own levels. These interviews can be valuable information in determining levels of valence and expectancy (Vroom, 1964). A coach should keep notes on the three aspects of Vroom's VIE during the interview sessions. Through these observations and interviews, a coach can rather objectively rank or rate the players in these various aspects.

RATING VALENCE AND EXPECTANCY

One objective method of measuring the valence and expectancy ratings is through a questionnaire.

Separate sections intended to rate valence and expectancy are built into the overall questionnaire design. The questions are multiple choice with the answers representing a continuum. Each response has a value. The total of the highest motivational answers of each aspect equals one. The player answering the questionnaire can choose a continuum of answers. (The questionnaire used in this study had five questions for both valence and expectancy.)

Coaches should exercise caution in treating the results of the questionnaire as absolute values. Bias may exist in the way questions are written and interpreted, as well as the propensity for people to answer these types of questions in a socially acceptable manner. (Cummings, 1989). Although questionnaires do not allow for the probe of additional information or allow for points of clarification, it is a useful research instrument whose implementation should be integrated with personal/video observations and interview process.

RATING INSTRUMENTALITY

The instrumentality of a player is derived from combining physical testing results with a coach's own evaluation of the player's defensive skill level. Agility sprint tests are the most accurate method in ranking athletes on a physical ability continuum.

Players can now be ranked according to their physical test results and perceived talent level. At this stage, the coach must estimate the intervals that realistically separate the athletes' instrumentality rating, keeping in mind that instrumentality can be considered a constant (e.g., value = 1) if all athletes are similar in this category.

Figure 1
Motivation = Valence x Instrumentality x Expectancy

Player	Valence	Instrumentality	Expectancy	VxIxE(Rank)	VxIxE
NC*	0.4	0.94	1.00	0.38(8)	0.40(8)
KD*	0.7	1.00	1.00	0.70(3)	0.70(4)
KE1	0.4	0.88	1.00	0.35(9)	0.40(8)
KE2*	0.9	0.86	1.00	0.77(2)	0.90(1)
LK	0.6	0.96	0.80	0.46(6)	0.48(7)
JL*	0.9	0.92	1.00	0.83(1)	0.90(1)
LL*	0.4	0.90	0.70	0.25(10)	0.28(10)
AP	0.2	0.82	0.60	0.10(11)	0.12(11)
CS	0.7	0.80	0.70	0.39(7)	0.49(6)
TT*	0.6	0.98	0.90	0.53(5)	0.54(5)
KW	0.8	0.84	1.00	0.67(4)	0.80(3)
Avg.	**0.6**	**0.9**	**0.88**	**0.49**	**0.55**

*denotes starting player
Data is from the Helix (Calif.) High School Girls' Volleyball Team during the 1990 season.

RESULTS

Figure 1 illustrates the instrumentality ratings and questionnaire results of the 1990 Helix High School girls' volleyball team. The VIE motivation product is also calculated with instrumentality rated as a constant (1.00). The intervals between the instrumentality ratings were set at 0.02 with the most athletic and skillful player getting the 1.0 rating.

A coach can record the results or interpretations in the same format as Figure 1. For the more subjective measures, this listing format in the chart will help make it easy to compare the players and assess if an accurate interpretation was made.

METHODS OF BEHAVIOR MODIFICATION

The methods of behavior modification include on-court and off-court training. Survey feedback is one method which gives players the results of the measurements and explains what the results mean. (Cummings, 1989). Be sure the players understand the aspects of motivation (e.g., valence, instrumentality, expectancy), but stress that the results are only estimations. It is possible the scores will vary as a result of an interpretation by a coach or player. Discuss the "whats" and "whys" of the interpretational differences with your team.

Group discussions, called team building (Cummings, 1989), are held to have the players discover how they can increase individual and team motivation in floor defense. The players need to learn for themselves what needs to be improved and how to solve these problems within the framework of the team. A block of time (e.g., minimum of one hour) should be spent in a classroom for the team building. The coach should be present and initiate the discussion, but then should allow the players to take over the direction of the group and remain quiet. There may be silent periods of more than 15 minutes before someone in the group steps forward to lead the discussion. Rest assured, though, a player in the group will eventually take the leadership role.

Besides these cognitive types of training, on-court drills should be designed to expand the desires (valence) and expectations of the players. Use creative scoring to improve the desires and expectations of the players. Bonus points can be given during drills for defensive efforts that exemplify the standards you have set for the team.

This "bonus point" concept can be implemented in random fashion or as part of the drill design. The drills should be constructed with the expectation of each ball being played. In addition, the coach should create a scoring system which encourages each player to make any and every dig.

A menu of drills which can accomplish this task are listed below:
• cooperative drills where two teams work together to keep the rally going;
• error-correction drills where the coach initiates the play, imitates where an error occurred and expects the player to make the dig before the drill continues;
• drills where earning a point is accomplished with a dig, but the dig itself is not the sole purpose of the drill (e.g., working on a quick attack).

RESULTS FROM EXPERIMENTATION

Individual defensive statistics for players on a high school girls' volleyball team were kept for 24 matches during the 1990 season. Statistics from the first 13 matches were documented prior to the behavior modification process; the remaining statistics were documented from 11 matches following the behavior modification process. The following behavior modification interventions were used in this study: survey feedback, team building, constant phased to random reinforcement and an honor/reward system for drills. These interventions occurred for a one-week period. There was no control group because the team needed to be treated as a complete unit.

The survey feedback and team building sessions were valuable because it forced the players to verbalize their own perceived defensive abilities. The VIE served as a framework for the survey feedback and team building discussions. During the survey feedback session, the validity of the questionnaire was discussed with specific regards to each question. Drills were designed with an honor/reward system in mind, using standards which increase the valence and expectancy of all team members.

Spreadsheets charting the number of successful digs during competition

According to Welch, the significance that can be drawn from studying the distribution of team dig opportunities lies in shedding light on the question, "Who is making the defensive saves?"

Photo: University of the Pacific

for each player were analyzed (see Figure 2). Besides keeping each individual player's dig total, the opponents' kill total was also documented. This data determined the total number of digging opportunities in a match for the high school. Opponent attack errors are not a factor in digging opportunities. This information was utilized to determine a team's floor defense efficiency by using the following formula:

$$\frac{\text{Digs}}{\text{Digs + Opponent's Kills}}$$

This percentage illustrates a team's ability to convert dig opportunities from every ball attacked into the playing area.

Further analysis shows the distribution of dig opportunities per each player/position/rotation. In a perfect volleyball world, each starting position should dig one-sixth (16.6-percent) of the total team digs. But volleyball is not played in an error-free vacuum and many variables affect this assumption. They include:
- two players sharing the same position during a match;
- opponent's hitting tendencies;
- defensive positioning dictated by the defensive system.

The significance that can be drawn from studying the distribution of team dig opportunities lies in shedding light on the question: Who is making the defensive saves on our side of the net?"

FINAL RESULTS

The research findings showed that after one week of behavior modification, team floor defense efficiency increased from 78.1-percent to 86.4-percent, a difference of more than eight percent (see Figures 2 and 3). This author concluded that the increase in defense efficiency (78.1-86.4) was significant, especially in relation to the short time period in which the behavior modification process was employed. The data also illustrated a more evenly distributed percentage of dig opportunities among the six positions on the court. This would suggest the players on the court taking a more active role in defense.

The validity and reliability of the results are certainly drawn into question, especially considering the short time period in which the experiment was conducted (21 days). In addition, unknown variables may have affected the experiment's findings, including strength of opponents. However, the research does represent a realistic time frame that a coach could devote to studying this aspect of the game, considering the time restrictions inherent with a high school season.

SUMMARY

Vroom's Expectancy Theory (VIE) is a valuable model for explaining the aspects of motivation in athletes. Taking the VIE framework a step further and applying it to floor defense demonstrates its value in analysis and giving direction for creating

Figure 2

Floor Defense Statistics
(Prior to Behavior Modification)

Players	Digs	%Team Digs
NC	15	11
KD	40	29
KE1	0	0
KE2	9	6
LK	0	0
JL	39	28
LL	14	10
AP	2	1
CS	0	0
TT	13	9
KW	7	5
Total	**139**	**99**

Opponents' Successful Attacks = 139
Opponents' Kills = 39
Total Playable Attacks = 178
Floor Defense Efficiency = 0.78

Figure 3

Floor Defense Statistics
(After Behavior Modification)

Players	Digs	%Team Digs
NC	21	17
KD	27	21
KE1	4	3
KE2	6	5
LK	2	2
JL	32	25
LL	14	11
AP	1	1
CS	0	0
TT	7	5
KW	13	10
Total	**127**	**100**

Opponents' Successful Attacks = 127
Opponents' Kills = 20
Total Playable Attacks = 147
Floor Defense Efficiency = 0.86

behavior modification plans. The methods described in this article will open communication lines between teammates and the coaching staff, encouraging players to evaluate situations and be effective decision-makers.

REFERENCE TEXT

Bertucci, Bob, Ed. (1987). *The AVCA Volleyball Handbook*, Indianapolis, IN: Masters Press.

Cummings, Thomas G. (1989). *Organization Development and Change.* St. Paul, MN: West Publishing Company.

Neville, William J. (1990). *Coaching Volleyball Successfully.* Champaign, IL: Leisure Press.

Vroom, Victor H. (1964). *Work and Motivation.* New York, N.Y.: John Wiley and Sons, Inc.

Mike Welch is the head women's coach at the University of North Florida (Jacksonville, Fla.) and is a USA Volleyball CAP Level III accredited coach.

Section VI: Drills

Transition Drills

This drill is designed to train your right-front (RF) and right-back (RB) players to coordinate and make good, quick transitions off your opponent's off-speed shots (mainly tips). This is especially needed if you run a rotational defense against a team without great outside hitters.

The RF must first block jump (see Figure 1). The coach tips the ball over the block. The RB digs the ball high enough so that the RF has time to turn and get under the ball and set to either the middle or the outside.

In a variation of this drill, the coach can replace the RB and simulate bad digs by tossing the ball in different areas at different heights and speeds. Challenge the RF by really varying the tosses. The RF will have to find the ball. run it down, and still make a good set, either overhand or underhand. Constant repetition will make your RF comfortable at making this play in a match. Making sure your hitters can get a good swing at the ball in your counterattack will lead to more points for your team.

This drill can also be run with a middle blocker (MB). If your RF player is your setter, add an MB who slides to the outside as both players block jump (see Figure 2). The coach tips over the block and the RB digs the ball. The MB must now get into position to attack (through either a quick or high set) and verbally communicate with the setter as to what she or he will hit. The setter (RF) sets either the MB or a high ball to the left-side hitter (see Figure 3).

The Transition Drill is needed if a team runs a rotational defense against a team without great outside hitters.

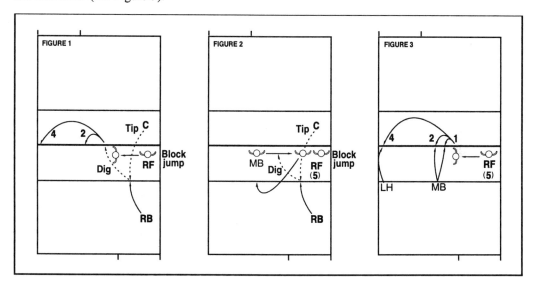

Tom Shoji is the head women's volleyball coach at the University of Southern Colorado (Pueblo, Colo.) and is a member of the USA Volleyball CAP Cadre.

Two Competitive Team Drills

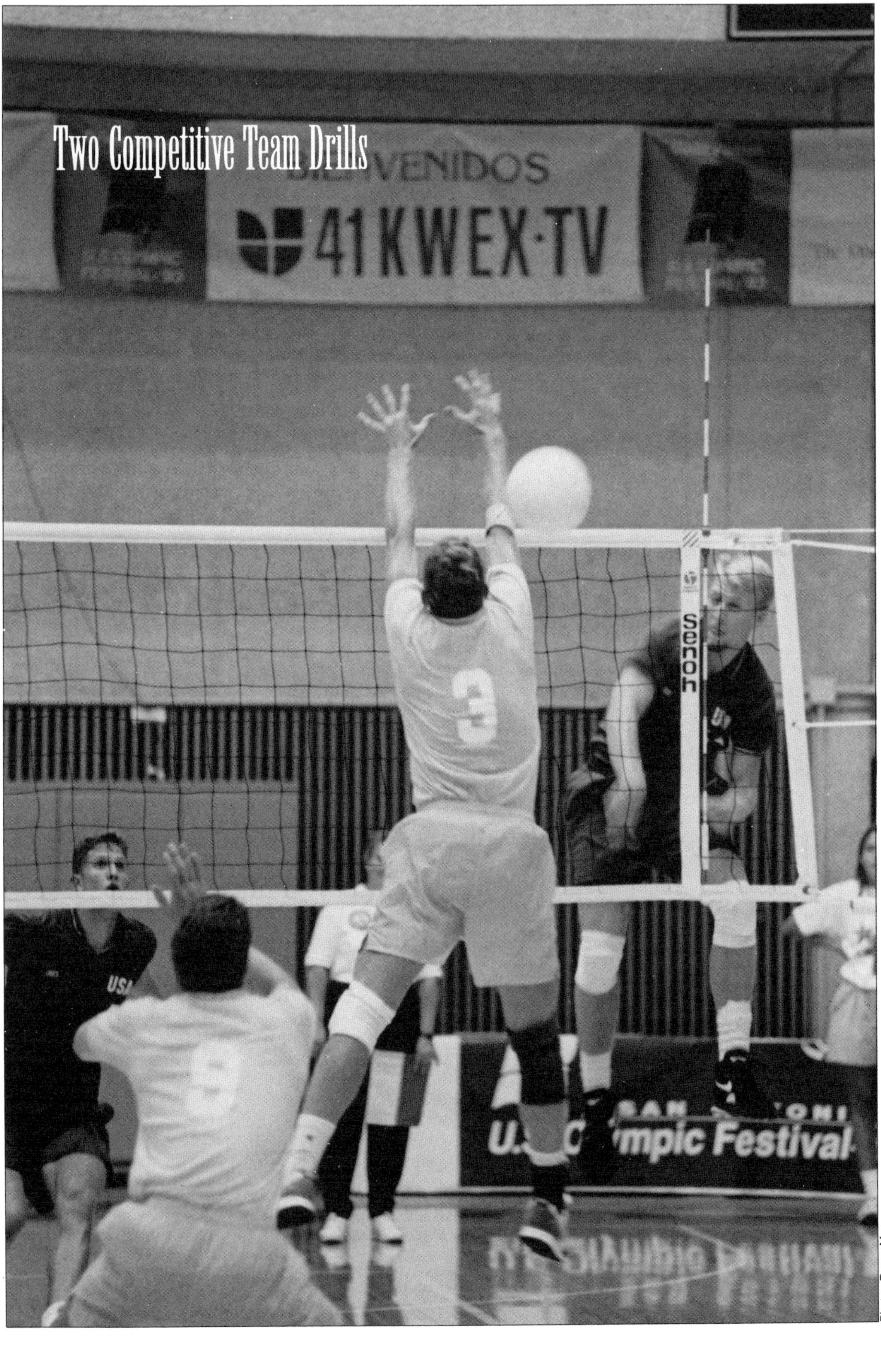

Photo: Roger Mar

Encouraging your team to compete during a match is an age-old pastime, but it takes more than encouragement to make a team play well. It all starts in the training gym, where the coach creates situations that encourage competitive behavior. Here are two examples of competitive team drills that create the desired atmosphere.

One drill places the focus simply on competing. Every point must be fought for and a resulting loss increases the athlete's desire not to let that happen again. This is the atmosphere that was created by the 1984 and '88 men's Olympic gold medal teams and is a good model for all of us to follow when preparing our teams to be successful.

The second drill is designed to train the server in a game situation and while under pressure. It is a drill to train servers and not the serving technique.

Encouraging a competitive team begins in the training gym and ends on the court during a match.

WASH POINT SCORING

In a generic sense, the term "wash" applies to any number of situations in everyday life. If two people spend a day together and one pays for a movie and the other the munchies, they tend to call it a wash — no one has gained and no one has lost. In volleyball, however, the term becomes somewhat more complicated.

In simple terms, wash means that no point has been scored. In wash scoring, points can be scored only after two rallies have been played. When the first rally is completed, a second rally is played with the other team now receiving the initial ball. When the second rally is over, it is then possible to determine which team has won the point or if indeed a point has been scored. (For a team to score a point, it must win both rallies. However, if each team wins one of the two rallies, then it is called a wash and no point is scored by either team (Iams, 1993).

THE SKINS GAME

The first drill is a scoring variation of the classic wash drill. The scoring is the same, only there are a few new wrinkles.

To review the wash drill scoring, both teams must score two "small" points in a row in order to score a "big" point (see Figure 1 on next page). One side is the serving team, the other is the receiving team. The serving team serves the ball and at the conclusion of the rally (including a missed serve), a second ball is tossed by the coach to the serving team and play is continued. A team scoring both times gains a big point. If one team scores on the serve and the other team scores on the free ball, a wash or no point is declared. The objective is three points by the receiving team and two points by the serving team and then a rotation occurs.

Now comes the variation. The objective is competition, so you must make the teams as equal as possible. The scoring stays the same for the small and big points, but they are now playing for six "giant" points.

In order to score a giant point, one team must win as both the serving team and the receiving team. In other words, when one team successfully wins the three points or two points, responsibilities are immediately changed in that same rotation (serving team becomes receiving team and receiving team becomes serving team). If there is a split, a wash is declared and the game

Figure 1

To Earn a Big Point:
•If the serving team wins rally from serve and wins rally of free ball toss from coach, serving team earns a big point.
•If the receiving team wins rally from the serve and wins rally of free ball toss to serving team, the receiving team gets one big point.

No Points (Wash)
•If serving team wins the rally from the serve and loses the rally from the free ball toss from the coach, no team scores (wash).
•If the serving team loses the rally from serve and wins the rally from the free ball toss, no team scores (wash).

To Earn a Giant Point
•One giant point is scored if one team scores serving and receiving consecutively. If no team does, giant point is added to the next round up to a max of six points. The serving team rotates when it scores two big points and the receiving team rotates when it scores two big points and the receiving team rotates when it scores three big points. If no team scores serving and receiving consecutively for all rotations, play a rally game to 15.

continues in the next rotation following the same procedure. (Note: It is suggested that a 2-2-1-2-2 rotation pattern is used to keep the players fresh). However, the next rotation is worth two points. So the previous giant point that was not acquired is then carried over in the same manner as in the now famous "Skins Game" in professional golf.

This same procedure continues with the strong possibility of the last rotation being worth six points. If there is a tie or there are carryover points remaining after all six rotations are completed, then one game to 15 is played using the rally-point scoring system for those points or to break the tie.

I always like to play for a little something, so I always have some sort of physical training exercise that nobody cares too much to do as the punishment or reward for the winning and losing team. This could be sprints, the running of stadium stairs, pushing the boards or towels multiple repetitions, a preconceived circuit of various exercises that would make a Marine cringe, etc. The idea is to make them want to fight so hard to win the match that they will never quit or concede a loss until the last point is scored.

The idea of physical training is not to hurt the athlete, so be very careful about your choice as the punishment for losing. You are trying to create a competitive atmosphere and add another element to the drill, not show off your sadistic, dark side. If you are too soft in what you are playing for you might lose the benefits of the hour-and-a-half of competition. It is my suggestion that the younger the athlete, the more careful you must be with this type of system. Possibly, the teams could be playing for ice cream or milk shakes and will accomplish the same results as physical exercise.

Another item you must consider when using this drill is that because this is a competitive drill, there will be a great deal of officiating going on by the players. Make sure you establish one person as the final arbiter on all questionable calls. My suggestion is the head coach is always the person who makes the call.

Like all drills, adapt this one to the level you are coaching. The element of competition is what you are after. Experiment with lower goals with the less-experienced players and as their skill level improves, increase the goals.

PING PONG SCORING

The idea for this drill came out of a desire to create a competitive serving atmosphere within the confines of a practice. I wanted to train servers, not the technique of serving. Multiple serving drills, for me, have never accomplished the game-like pressure that I would like my athletes working under in practice. If an athlete serves at a chair in the corner of the court for 15 minutes, that is great for teaching technique. But how is that same athlete going to react when the match is on the line and there needs to be a good, quality serve?

Thus, I came up with the idea of scrimmaging using a ping pong method of scoring. This is simply a rally-point game or match, but each server on both teams serves five balls consecutively before there is a rotation by both squads.

The reason for five balls is that each successive ball has a little more pressure being placed on the server. (Note: I have also experimented with three balls per server. This did not accomplish the same pressure effect on the server, but it did shorten the time for the drill. I now use it as a one game, end-of-the-practice drill to practice both serving and rally point game situations). Since a point is scored on each serve, the server has to concentrate on hitting that quality serve or the other team will side-out with ease, scoring at will. (Note: The more equally matched the teams are the more competitive this drill will be. This is, however, a great first team versus second team drill because of the rally-point scoring system. Anyone can score on each serve).

I have played the game to various point totals. The point total that has produced the best results is 45. You may be thinking that there may not be a full rotation if there is such a low point total. You are right! That is why when one game is completed, you change sides and start in the rotation you ended with using the same server who just completed his turn. Play can be a best of five match or a number of predetermined games.

Remember, serving to chairs or positions on the court for multiple repetitions is a way to train the technique of serving. Placing the pressure on the server in gamelike situations trains servers.

According to Read, coaches must adapt all drills to the level they are coaching. The element of competition is what you are after.

REFERENCES

Iams, J. (1993). *Competitive Volleyball Drills and Scoring Systems*. Ames, IA: Championship Books and Video Productions, 6.

Tom Read is a physical education instructor in California's Saddleback Valley Unified School District (Fresno, Calif.) and a is charter member of the USA Volleyball CAP Cadre.

Volleyball Mini-Games and Movement Training

Volleyball Mini-Games and Movement Training

DON SHONDELL
JOEL WALTON

NCAA restrictions limiting the organized volleyball training period to 22 weeks have created a need for incorporating competitive play in the off-season that will motivate players to work their hardest while still having fun. Competitive mini-games meet that requirement.

These games utilize a smaller court, involve fewer players on a team and incorporate rule modifications that involve rotation and eligibility of certain positions to attack the ball from in front of the attack line. All modifications of the regular six-on-six game have a specific purpose for developing certain skills under a competitive but unsupervised environment.

Because the play in these situations is unofficiated, the players must exhibit an attitude of fairness at all times. If the opponent's attack is too close to clearly call out, then call it in. If you could not tell, replay the point. If a player touches the net or the ball as it is sailing out, call it. This way, players will gain the respect of teammates and coaches and keep the game rolling on a positive plane.

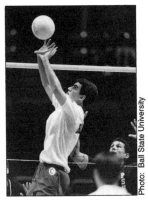

According to Shondell, mini-games develop a number of skills under a competitive but unsupervised environment.

In addition, the off-season is an opportunity to learn to know teammates better on the court. On some days, it is best to mix young and old players. On other days, to toughen up competition, it is better to divide players into two or three leagues based on relative strength. Captains need to make these decisions in terms of long-range development.

Undeniably, the competitive games have different purposes and need to be conducted differently on certain days to result in a totally skilled player with a positive attitude toward teammates and team leaders.

TWO-ON-TWO HALF-COURT GAMES

An excellent mini-game to incorporate into off-season play is the two-on-two (half-court) game, which is best played on a smaller court. The small court encourages longer rallies and forces a more controlled game in all aspects. Also, the small court (15 x 30) divides a 30 x 30 area into two playing courts, allowing two games to be played simultaneously. (On a full-sized court, the opportunities to rally are minimized because of the defender's need to cover 900 square feet of the court.) Therefore, the major benefit of the two-on-two half-court game is that it allows more opportunities to pass and serve in a competitive situation.

SHORT AND NARROW COURT/NO SPIKING/THREE HITS ON A SIDE

The two-on two game is a ball control game that requires many overhand passing contacts and is excellent for non-setters who need overhand practice. The competitive aspect also makes the practice more goal-oriented.

In addition, modifications can be made to this particular mini-game, such as utilizing the short court or allowing no spiking. In this game, the ball must be angled upward as it crosses the net to lengthen the rallies. The court is 30 feet deep and 15 feet wide. Tape is put down to divide the volleyball court in half, and an antenna put up to divide the net into two courts. The attack line becomes the baseline. Also, permit only forearm

110

Obviously, many of the skills developed and honed in the mini-games can be translated to the six-on-six contest during the regular season.

and overhand passing. In theory, the first pass should be forearm and the next two overhand.

During the "no spiking" game, many opportunities are provided to overhand pass the ball. The game encourages the setter to be aware of where the opponent is on defense, as well as the vulnerable areas of the court. Short sets of a hairpin variety just over the net and sets near the sideline between defenders and deep, quick sets into the court's deep corners magnify the difficulty of the exercise. Players must rotate but are allowed to switch to balance the court during rallies. (During service, the ball may be either served or easily tossed across the net. The purpose of the serve is to initiate play, not score points.)

TWO-ON-TWO/HALF-COURT/DEEP HIT

This mini-game is great for developing skills in scoring, passing, setting, back-court attacking and digging. The court is 15x 30, as in the previously described no spike games. In this game, the serving should be strong (you may wish to award two points for an ace). To keep all courts finishing at approximately the same time, a 15- or 21-point rally game or a 15-minute timed gamed is suggested.

Because the object in the off-season is to develop all-around skill, players may be restricted from specializing in this mini-game. Whoever serves will also be the passer. The other player becomes the setter and the passer the attacker (from behind the attack line). The opponents both drop back to dig and the non-digger sets. It is sometimes wise to penalize a spiking error by awarding the defense two points instead of the usual one. This encourages offensive accuracy. Finally, blocking is not allowed in two-on-two deep hit.

During the "deep hit" game, the attacker must take off from behind the attack restraining line. This promotes controlled hitting and, as a result, provides more opportunities to dig a ball in the back court since this modification allows the digger greater preparation time in preparing to dig the back.

Another modification involves prohibiting the block in order to force the ball to be dug. Any soft shots must land beyond the 3-meter line or be completely eliminated, except on broken plays. The soft shots must then be hit to midcourt in a playable manner.

As in the previous games, rule modifications can be made to this mini-game. For example:

•Allow all players to attack from the front row, but all off-speed shots or setter tips must land behind the 3-meter line. Hard spikes, however, may be spiked straight down. It is the blocker's job to prevent this from happening.

•Allow only the left side player to hit and the right front set, advocating pure rotation of positions with no specialization. This allows each player to gain skill in playing each position.

THREE-ON-THREE/TWO BLOCKERS

Three-on-three is best played on a long, narrow court, regular depth, 15-foot width. The major value of this game is that it forces the attacker to hit against a tight two-player block.

The ideal structure is to allow only one hitter, one setter and one passer, playing the position to which they just rotated. The server becomes the passer/digger, the left front blocks and hits in that position and the right front becomes the setter/blocker on the right side. Everything is done without restriction, except soft shots that land in front of the attack line are prohibited. Finger tips may not be used for soft shots, and the ball must be spiked or rolled across the net and land beyond the attack line.

There are several benefits of three-on-three games, including forcing the hitter to exploit the weak blocker by hitting off or over the hands; allowing the hitter to work on the high reach hit, wipe off and drive shot attacks; practicing the soft roll (having it land beyond the 3-meter line and rolling it across rather than tipping); learning play deflection in the back row; and practicing covering blocked balls by the attack team.

In addition to the benefits, the tactics of the three-on-three game are varied. Offensively, the hitter is to hit any set the setter can set anywhere along the net. The hitter, setter and passer must all be ready to cover and replay the blocked ball. Defensively, since there is no cross-court in which to sharply angle the ball, the back-row player should remain near the baseline to dig the over-the-block shot or the deflected drive shot hit deep off the court. The blockers must get off the net and play every ball deflected up or off the court within 10 feet of the net. Also, the blockers must be aware of their outside hand position to avoid being tooled. If they see the hitter start to angle the body away from the court, keep (or pull) the outside hand down. This drill provides concentrated opportunities for the blockers to get many chances to block in a controlled format. Because the hitter is always close to the setter, it is then easier for the blocker to focus on both the setter and the hitter when blocking. The narrowness of the court forces the hitter to challenge the block and virtually every ball hit will be deflected, giving the defense (blockers and diggers) an opportunity to play deflections and then convert to offense.

As before, a number of modifications can be utilized to enhance the game. For example, allow specialization and setter tips. In this modification, the game becomes easier for the offense and more difficult for the defense. The offensive team is permitted to allow all three players to hit and the setter may tip anywhere, forcing the blocker and deep defensive player to concentrate first on the setter's attack and then on the attacker.

Or, a different modification forces the passer, when attacking, to take off from behind the restraining line (as if he/she were a back-row player).

The rationale for such modifications is two-fold. First, allowing everyone to hit as front-row players provides an offensive option that is in use in the six-player game when the front-row player drops back to pass. Secondly, the back-row attack is the aspect of the six-player game when the passer is a back-row player.

In summary, three-on-three is a game allowing the two units of three to receive a maximum of game-like offensive and blocking opportunities. It focuses offensively on working against a block, a phase of hitting often neglected. It focuses on the wipe-off and drive shot, as well as providing many opportunities to serve, pass and set.

FOUR-ON-FOUR

The four-on-four games may be played on a narrow (15 x 30) or regular (30 x 30) court. On the narrow court, opportunity is provided to work on overload blocking —three blockers working against four hitters in a confined 15-foot net area. A tight, well-controlled block becomes mandatory. The offense, to be effective, must employ time delay plays—tandems and individual stunts—to throw off the timing of the blockers. The wipe off and drive shots are essential, as well as a deceptive roll shot that must come down behind the attack line unless touched by the blockers.

On the full court, the four-on-four game incorporates more one-on-one and open net hitting, thus opening up the opportunity to dig the hard spike. It places an emphasis on reading the setter and hitter and adjusting before the hit to the proper digging position.

The objective of these modifications is to allow only one-on-one blocking with three diggers. It also gives everyone an opportunity to play each position on offense and defense. On defense, one player up front blocks while the other drops off to dig the opposite sideline. Soft shots on or in front of the 3-meter line are not permitted.

Offensive tactics vary, but in four-player (played under the "all players eligible to hit" system), all players will be attacking at the net. The normal three-hitter offense can be practiced with two players running quickly and the passer swinging right or left inside for the play set. Defense against the above offense requires a formation of three blockers at the net and a back court player who must be ready for anything. The object is to get two blockers on every play and dig the two sidelines. The blockers must protect the center of the court.

In the four-on-four deep hit game, all attacking must be done by taking off from behind the attack line. This game should require one blocker on defense and three diggers. The setter may move back after setting with the attacker blocking or the setter can remain at the net and block. (Variations can bring more challenge to the game. For example, on transition,

Eventually, off-season play will be a memory and the time to execute on the court with six players will be at hand.

the blocker may hit quick from in front of the attack line, but everyone else must hit from behind the attack line. No players may cause a soft shot to land on or in front of the attack line. This variation allows a tall blocker to move to the net and then work on quick hitting in transition.)

The six-on-six game should allow more balls to be dug and longer rallies, but it will result in an unequal number of contacts by the competitors and certainly fewer opportunities to serve for each player.

In summary, the four-on-four game is similar to the six-player game, but allows more opportunities for each of the players to handle the ball. Offensively, it allows three-hitter plays to be run and also allows the setter to attack the ball as long as the ball comes down beyond the 3-meter line. It puts a premium on the blockers reading the setter and the hitting and blocking at the net. It also demands that the non-blockers get off the net quickly to dig the crosscourt shot.

FIVE-ON-FIVE

The five-on-five game can be played with either three front-row players or three back-row players. If three front-row players are used, one must be the setter and defensively all three are eligible to block. It places two diggers in the back court, one digging line and the other middle back and the opposite blocker moving off the net to dig crosscourt.

The main advantage of the game is that it forces the non-blocker to practice getting off the net quickly in order to dig the cross-court shot. Also, in the game that allows only two front-row players and the setter coming up from the back row, only two hitters will be hitting against two blockers at the net and three diggers. There will be a lot of one-on-one blocking and a lot of opportunities to dig.

A variation in the three-up game is to maintain rotation order and have whoever is right front set. This allows everyone to work on all of the skills. In the two-player system, specialize the setter and when in the front row, have one eligible front-court hitter, but three back-row attackers.

SIX-ON-SIX

The six-on-six game should allow more balls to be dug and longer rallies, but it will result in an unequal number of contacts by the competitors and certainly fewer opportunities to serve for each player. In six-player volleyball, there is a need for understanding the parameters of your position (what is your responsibility and what is your teammate's?). A good six-on-six player is disciplined and able to focus on every action by the opponents. If there are problems in execution, concentrate solely on the process. Forget the product! If a player is able to focus on the next opportunity and execute correctly, the outcome will take care of itself.

Because of the closeness on the court to your teammates, relay the importance of controlling negative emotions. Teach the players to work to remain poised and focused, regardless of the previous play. The trademark of a champion is the ability to deal with both success and failure. Six-player volleyball, in particular, is a psychologically challenging game.

Once you learn how the skills are to be executed and what your role is on the court, it is just a matter of staying focused on what is likely to happen next and never allowing any incident on the court to affect concentration. This should be your attitude every time you walk on any court, whether to practice or to compete.

Eventually, off-season play will be a memory and the time to execute on the court with six players will be at hand. Therefore, in the six-on-six scrimmage situation, communication is very important, along with mental toughness and determination to make the play. Players need to be positive catalysts who are always ready to make the next play and are always encouraging teammates, regardless of the situation. In blocking, have players give the blocking signal and help teammates prepare mentally and physically for the next play. Always remember, steady pressure on the opponent is the key to success. A championship team is always the result of these two factors. They are summarized in the phrase mental toughness. The mind controls the body! Loss of self-control always results in the loss of physical control.

These are the things both coaches and players must concentrate on in six-on-six games. Accentuate the positive and eliminate the negative. Concentrate on process, not the product.

Don Shondell, Ph.D., is the head men's volleyball coach at Ball State University. Joel Walton is the assistant men's volleyball coach at the institution.

Bonusball

Bonusball

This drill should be used when a practice session has a high percentage of emphasis on defense. I designed the drill initially to train a young setter to practice making decisions on critical plays. I found that to some degree that was effective, but it quickly became clear that it could also be effective for improving defensive effort.

I particularly like this drill for several reasons:

• Players are motivated to execute, as there is an advantage in being the first team to earn their bonusball.

• Players learn that while all rallies are important, one needs to practice making "percentage" decisions on crucial plays.

• Players will quickly learn to put their mistakes behind them.

• Some of the best defensive efforts of the season are demonstrated in this drill.

• Coaches are involved and can push all players in a sometimes stressful situation.

According to Dearing, players will quickly learn to put their mistakes behind them after engaging in this drill.

SET-UP

Two coaches begin off court near the 3-meter line. Each coach has three volleyballs and one colored volleyball — the "bonusball." A basket of extra volleyballs is placed between the coaches.

DRILL DESIGN

Each team starts in its defensive alignment in the first rotation. Each rally is initiated by a toss or attack from the coach opposite them (ranging from an easy free ball to a difficult down ball). The winner of each rally wins the next ball. The first team to win three rallies gets their "bonusball." A team must win the rally on its "bonusball" to win a rotation. The first team to win six rotations wins the drill. If a team wins a rally on its "bonusball" rally, then play stops and they quickly rotate while their opponent stays in the same rotation. If a team loses its "bonusball" rally, then it receives balls from the basket on each rally it wins until the opponent earns its "bonusball" and a chance to win a rotation. If neither team wins a "bonusball," then neither team rotates and the drill begins again.

VARIATIONS

1. The "Goller" version (named for the player who suggested it) allows the first team that receives the "bonusball" the opportunity to get a second chance by winning three more rallies before their opponent earns its first "bonusball." This does tend to keep both teams concentrating on each play.

2. When one team wins a rotation, both teams rotate. In a game, we often have rotations that produce more points than others, so this varia-

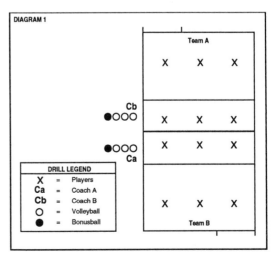

DIAGRAM 1

Team A

X X X

Cb
●○○○   X X X

●○○○   X X X
Ca

DRILL LEGEND
X = Players
Ca = Coach A
Cb = Coach B
○ = Volleyball
● = Bonusball

X X X

Team B

tion allows that to happen in the drill.

3. If the coach considers one team stronger than the other: the weaker team may only need to win one rally to get their "bonusball" and the stronger team may only play in their three weakest rotations or the three rotations that produced the least number of points in the previous match.

Joel Dearing is the head volleyball coach at Springfield College (Springfield, Mass.), and is a member of the USA Volleyball CAP Cadre.

The Run-Through

The run-through is used in many aspects of volleyball. Defensively, when a player needs to play a tip, a roll shot or ball hit off the block, the run-through is a more efficient movement to the ball than going to the floor. A run-through is also used on service reception for the extremely short serve. The movement itself is executed with both arms together, extended up and out while playing the ball on the run. The player should not try to stop before or during contact, but continue through. By dropping the appropriate shoulder, the player can angle his/her platform to redirect the ball to the target.

By dropping the appropriate shoulder, a player can angle his/her platform to redirect the ball to the target.

Photo: University of Hawai'i

Through the years, my team has changed from the small, quick player to the taller, slower player. We have found that run-throughs help improve our overall defense. By using run-throughs, and not going to the floor so often, the taller, slower player can transition more quickly from defense. The run-through also speeds up our transition offense by providing a little more impetus to the ball causing it to get to the setter quicker.

To teach the run through you need to be sure to encourage your players to touch the ball but not go to the floor if the ball is within their reach. You will find the more positive you are in reinforcing that touch, the more they will begin to reach balls with both hands. Young players also like the run-throughs when they realize that they do not have to go to the floor all of the time. I have seen many high school teams improve their movement skills greatly by utilizing the run-through.

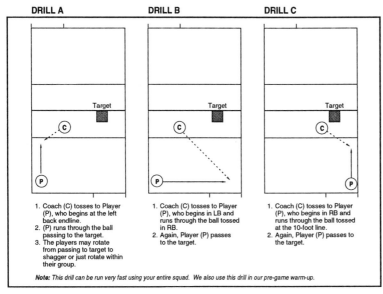

DRILL A

1. Coach (C) tosses to Player (P), who begins at the left back endline.
2. (P) runs through the ball passing to the target.
3. The players may rotate from passing to target to shagger or just rotate within their group.

DRILL B

1. Coach (C) tosses to Player (P), who begins in LB and runs through the ball tossed in RB.
2. Again, Player (P) passes to the target.

DRILL C

1. Coach (C) tosses to Player (P), who begins in RB and runs through the ball tossed at the 10-foot line.
2. Again, Player (P) passes to the target.

Note: This drill can be run very fast using your entire squad. We also use this drill in our pre-game warm-up.

Brenda Williams is the head women's coach at Olivet Nazarene University (Bourbannais, Ill.) and is a USA Volleyball CAP Level I accredited coach.

What is the AVCA?

The mission of the American Volleyball Coaches Association is to advance the development of the sport of volleyball by providing coaches with educational programs, a forum for opinion exchange and recognition opportunities. Member participation is vital to the association accomplishing this mission.

The following principles guide the AVCA in the attainment of its goals: To maintain a membership group representative of all levels of competition; to promote the game of volleyball within the general philosophical framework of education; to encourage participation within the highest standards of competition; and to develop greater interest, understanding and support of the sport.

HISTORY OF THE AVCA

In 1981, the AVCA was incorporated as a private non-profit 501-(c)-3 educational corporation. The original Board of Directors consisted of eight NCAA Division I collegiate coaches. A part-time executive director administered the programs.

As the AVCA began to grow and diversify, a full-time executive director was hired in July 1983. An associate director was hired in April 1986 and an administrative assistant in September 1988.

In August 1992, the association moved from San Mateo, Calif., to Colorado Springs, Colo. The staff has increased to the following positions: executive director, director of membership services, assistant director of membership services, director of sports information, director of publishing, sports information assistant and part-time accountant. In addition, the association employs interns and other part-time people.

In 1986, the Board was increased to 13 members, and in 1987 and 1989, the Board was increased to enfranchise first the high school and then the junior communities.

Membership increased steadily from 1981 through 1987 (about 150 new members per year), followed by a 106 percent boom in 1988. Since 1986, high school membership has more than tripled. High school coaches from 46 states and the District of Columbia are members. At the collegiate level, all major NCAA conferences are represented and membership among the club coaches has risen dramatically.

The original members of the AVCA were all intercollegiate coaches who banned together to unite this particular coaching body. They have been the backbone of the association's existence and a united voice determining volleyball's future.

Perhaps the most significant decision was made at the San Francisco convention in 1986, however, when the membership recognized the growing and developing high school and club communities. The name of the association was changed to reflect these growing constituencies. From the original Collegiate Volleyball Coaches Association, the American Volleyball Coaches Association was born with the intent of responding to and serving all volleyball coaches.

SERVICE FUNCTIONS

The AVCA services its members through more varied functions than almost any other coaches' organization. The AVCA only involves itself with activities that best exemplify the image of amateur athletics. Its ultimate mission is to enhance the image and increase awareness for the sport of volleyball. Listed below are summaries of just some of the many AVCA activities:

1. The AVCA serves as the main liaison between its members and the NCAA for sport legislation. This role is vital in that the AVCA communicates members' beliefs and opinions on issues affecting volleyball and its participants.

2. The AVCA prepares, edits and distributes 12 monthly newsletters and six professional journals to all of its members. Associate members receive 12 news-

letters/drill bulletins that deal with issues affecting high school and juniors coaches. College members receive a weekly publication during the season that covers the ongoing results and activities of teams around the country.

3. The AVCA orchestrates a series of awards programs which recognize the competitive efforts of more than 325 student-athletes and coaches. These programs include acknowledging athletes at the regional/district levels, as well as on the national level. These programs are for all Division levels and are as listed:

•For NCAA Division I

Eight (8) All-District Teams - 1st and 2nd: 12 members each

•For NCAA Division II

Eight (8) All-Region Teams - 1st and 2nd: 12 members each

•For NCAA Division III

Eight (8) All-Region Teams - 1st and 2nd: 12 members each

•For NCAA Divisions I, II, III, NAIA & Junior College/Community College:

All-America Teams - 24 recipients each

National "Player of the Year" - 5 recipients

Coaches "Victory Club" Award

National "Coach of the Year" - 5 recipients

Region "Coach of the Year "- 8 (Div II), 8 (Div III), 9 (NAIA),

8 (JC/CC)

District "Coach of the Year" - 8 (Div I)

•For Men

All-America Teams - 18 recipients

National "Player of the Year"

Coaches "Victory Club" Award

National "Coach of the Year"

4. The AVCA organizes and conducts an annual convention and clinic for all its membership in conjunction with the NCAA Division I Women's Volleyball Championship.

5. The AVCA actively prepares and develops clinics, seminars and workshops for the professional development of its constituency.

6. The AVCA promotes and increases the media exposure of volleyball. The founding of the U.S. Volleyball Media Association, in cooperation with USA Volleyball, is a major step toward involving media in its own network. In addition, the AVCA is a member of the College Sports Information Directors of America and delivers presentations to that group.

7. The AVCA has written a National Volleyball Statistics Manual & Video and has been the primary force in developing a consistent method of compiling volleyball statistics.

8. Until 1994, the AVCA compiled and publicized all individual and team statistical information for every Division I school on a weekly basis and monthly for every Division II, III and NAIA school throughout the women's season. Upon compilation of statistics by the NCAA in 1994, the AVCA ceased this activity except for the NAIA.

9. The AVCA coordinates the polling of coaches weekly for ranking of the Top 25 teams in Division I; the Top 25 in Division II; the Top 15 in Division III and Division I men's; and the Top 10 in Division III men's volleyball. The Division I men's and women's polls are carried by USA TODAY. The other polls are carried by the AP Sports Stats Wire and major papers.

10. The AVCA administered the National Invitational Volleyball Championship, a 20-team Division I championship for institutions that were not selected to the NCAA championship. Through close contacts with all conference offices, the NIVC became a premier event for up and coming teams.

Other Educational Resources Available

The American Volleyball Coaches Association, in conjunction with USA Volleyball, the National Governing Body for the sport in the United States, is proud to offer a number of excellent educational publications through Volleyball Informational Products, a joint program of the two organizations

In addition to *The Best of Coaching Volleyball, Book Two: The Advanced Elements of the Game*, the following educational publications are also available:

The AVCA Volleyball Handbook
The Best of Coaching Volleyball, Book One: The Basic Elements of the Game
The Best of Coaching Volleyball, Book Three: The Related Elements of the Game (available Spring 1996)
Cadre Collection Volume II
The Coaches Guide to Beginning Volleyball Programs
Coaching Volleyball Successfully
Critical Thinking on Setter Development
Pass, Set, Crush
Rookie Coaches Guide
The Science of Coaching Volleyball
Strength Training and Conditioning for Volleyball

Also, the following periodicals are available:
American Volleyball (official AVCA newsletter, 12 issues per year)
Coaching Volleyball (official AVCA technical journal, six issues per year)
Power Tips (high school/junior drill bulletin, 12 issues per year)
Volleyball USA (USA Volleyball official magazine, four issues per year)

Finally, there is also an extensive video library available. The videos included in the collection explore all aspects of volleyball at levels ranging from beginner to advanced. Some of the nation's finest volleyball coaches provide expert technical direction.

For more information on any of these educational resource materials, please contact the AVCA office at (719) 576-7777, ext. 104.